Published for

The Co-operative Wholesale Society Limited

P.O. Box 53, New Century House,
Manchester M60 4ES

by The Sales Machine Limited

Edited by Sarah Charles
Designed by Applied Creativity Limited
Printed by Hazell Watson and Viney Limited

D1513341

Baking Your Cake & Eating it

100 Baking Recipes

Edited by
Sarah Charles

CO OP

Contents

Section
I

Serve a Savoury Special

Contents

Section 2

Make the Money go Round

Contents

Section
3

Give Them a Sweet Surprise

Contents

Section
4

Try a Treat for Teatime

The book you
helped us to write . . .

We at the Co-op feel proud of this little book for several reasons. As far as we're concerned it's something very new and exciting. And we hope that you, our shoppers, are going to feel the same way about it too.

To begin with, it's the first time we've produced a proper cookery paperback. Of course you will remember the three booklets on *Making the Most of Meat* which we published a little while ago. These were a great hit with all of you. So we thought it was about time we had a go at something more ambitious.

There was no problem at all about deciding what to do next. Because we had run a home-baking competition in a national newspaper, and the entries came flooding in giving your favourite recipes from all over the country.

The standard of these entries was so high that we've had no hesitation at all in keeping to our plan to publish a selection of the winners in this book.

But, being the Co-op and therefore always concerned about adding that extra bit more value for our shoppers, we also decided to make this a book that would be a real help to you in stretching the family food budget. So we asked our own Co-op kitchens to give us *their* favourite recipes too—good, basic ones that would satisfy hungry families without costing too much money or effort.

All the recipes in this book are prepared in the oven, and that makes them even more economical. As you know, you can use the oven to prepare a whole family meal at once. It cuts down quite a bit on your gas or electricity bills when you cook this way. And oven-baked meals can really be a treat—say, tasty bacon and egg pie to start with, a rich casserole full of good, slow-cooked meat and vegetables, and a tempting fruit pudding to round it off . . . delicious!

If you have another look at the list of contents on pages 4–7, you'll see that we've divided the book into four sections. Each section contains more than twenty recipes, all listed alphabetically.

The first section covers mostly main-course dishes. Several of these are quite unusual. Roasted Fruity Lamb, for instance, is an attractive variation of the weekend joint—as well as being a good way to make it go further. Gypsy Pie is an example of an old-fashioned dish. Tattee 'Oggie is a version of that West Country dish well-known to everyone—Cornish Pasty. But until you've made one yourself (especially this one) you haven't tasted the real thing. Our favourite in this section is Cheese Meringue Pie: the writer tells us it's a French convent feast-day treat—and it certainly is a feast!

The second section is full of really clever ideas for using inexpensive ingredients in ways that will surprise your family—and you too. Several of the recipes don't use meat at all and yet are really satisfying—Macaroni Slices, for example, or Cheesy Leek Flan. Then there's a super Mushroom and Celery Pie— from our only *male* winner in the competition. Others, like the delightfully descriptive Pensioner's Casserole, use handy 'standby' foods —in this case bacon and rice. Many of these recipes are very quick to prepare, too. And what about Cheese Whispers or Sage and Onion Pudding if you want a good idea to stretch a main meal further?

The third section contains puddings that are a real inspiration. Just to read the list of titles makes you want to start baking. Peach and Plenty Pudding, for instance, or Apple Almond Pie. Then there's a traditional Harvest Pudding, made at threshing time in the Midlands, and Baked Alaska, a sensational combination of hot pudding filled with ice-cream, which impresses everyone and yet is so easy to do.

The final section contains a wonderful selection of cakes and biscuits, from the simplest cookies to the most unusual continental specialities. One of them—Wacky Cake—comes all the way from Malaya, and was so christened by the sender because, she says, it breaks all the baking rules. The original recipe for Siena Cake was coaxed out of a waiter on an Italian holiday, while Gugelhuff is a version of a cake much enjoyed throughout Germany and Austria. And two of the best are traditional English: the rich fruit cake without which no Christmas or birthday party would be quite right and the superb Christmas Bunloaves recipe, which has been handed down in the writer's family for over eighty years.

There were others too, not included because their recipes were not for baked dishes. So perhaps we can carry on this idea and feature them in another book soon. But that depends on you. If you enjoyed this book and would like to see more like it, do let us know. After all, it is *your* Co-op, isn't it?

Sarah Charles
New Century House
Manchester
May 1973

Serve a Savoury Special

All the main dish recipes in this section are for good hearty family meals. Lots of them are your own tried and trusted favourites, in many cases for traditional and regional specialities.

Bacon and Egg Pie (Serves 4)

(From Mrs. Renee Parkinson, Doncaster, Yorks., a variation on a well-known favourite—but with unusual pastry)

Filling:
6 oz. grated cheese
¼ pint milk
¼ pint single cream
seasoning
2–3 rashers bacon
2 eggs

Rolled oat pastry:
1 oz. porridge oats
4 oz. plain flour
1 oz. margarine
1 oz. lard
1 egg yolk
pinch salt
water to mix

1. Sieve flour and salt, add oats, rub in margarine and lard until mixture resembles fine breadcrumbs. Mix to firm dough with egg yolk and a little water. **2.** Grill bacon lightly and chop. **3.** Line casserole dish with pastry. **4.** Beat eggs, add milk, cream, grated cheese, bacon, and seasoning. **5.** Pour carefully into pastry case and bake at mark 5 (375° F.) for about 35–45 minutes until set firm and top a golden brown.

Chicken Cooked in Cider

(Serves 4–5)

(From Mrs. V. Smith, Waddon, Croydon, Surrey, who says it is one of her family's favourites)

---

4 chicken legs
1 pint cider
1 large onion
2 bay leaves
2 cooking apples
2 tablespoons cooking oil

1 oz. dark brown sugar
salt and pepper
seasoned flour
1 lb. Patna rice
1 packet freeze dried peas

---

1. Skin chicken legs and coat with seasoned flour. **2.** Put cooking oil in large frying pan; when hot fry chicken pieces until golden brown on both sides, then place in large oven dish. **3.** While chicken browns, cut, wash, and slice onions; peel, core, and thinly slice apples. Fry onion in frying pan until golden brown, then add cider, bay leaves, salt, and pepper to taste. Simmer 20 minutes. **4.** Lay sliced apples over chicken and sprinkle brown sugar over top. Pour cider mixture over. **5.** Cook in a moderate oven mark 5 (375° F.) for about 1½ hours. **6.** Half an hour before dish is ready, put rice and peas together in plenty of boiling salted water and simmer until cooked. Serve with chicken.

Cheese Meringue Pie

(From Mrs. K. Halton, St. Helens, Lancs., who describes it as a French convent feast-day treat and delicious served cold with salad)

1 cooked flan case,
  approximately 7 inches
1 oz. butter
1 oz. plain flour
½ pint milk
6 oz. grated Cheddar cheese
2 egg yolks
salt and pepper
a little cayenne pepper

Topping:
2 egg whites
2 oz. grated Cheddar cheese
pinch salt

1. Melt butter in pan, stir in flour and fry gently without allowing to colour, for a few minutes. **2.** Gradually stir in milk, a little at a time. Bring the sauce to the boil, stirring and allow to cook gently for 2–3 minutes. Add cheese, egg yolks and seasoning. **3.** Pour into prepared flan case. **4.** Whisk egg whites and salt until stiff and fold in cheese. Cover pie with meringue and bake in moderate oven mark 4 (350° F.) for 20 minutes.

Beef and Batter Pudding

(Serves 4)

¼ lb. plain flour
pinch salt
1 standard egg
½ pint milk
1 tablespoon butter (melted)

½ packet sage and onion stuffing
½ lb. lean minced beef
2 oz. butter

---

1. Sift together flour and salt, add egg, ¼ pint milk, and butter and beat well. Stir in remaining milk. **2.** Make up stuffing according to directions on pack. Mix together prepared stuffing and minced beef and season well. Shape into small balls and place in 10 × 12-inch baking tin. Pour batter over. **3.** Bake at mark 7 (425° F.) for 20 minutes then reduce to mark 6 (400° F.) for a further 20 minutes.

Tripe Casserole

(Serves 4)

(From Miss R. Lord, Redbridge, Ilford, Essex)

1½ lb. cooked tripe
¼ pint approx. cooking oil
¼ pint approx. vinegar
1 onion (chopped)
2 oz. butter
½ lb. mushrooms

1 small tin tomatoes—liquid
  made up to ¾ pint with stock
  or water
1 oz. flour
1 oz. breadcrumbs
2 carrots (peeled and
  chopped)

1. Cut cooked tripe into strips and leave in enough oil and vinegar to cover for about 1 hour. **2.** Fry onion and carrots in 1 oz. butter. Peel and slice mushrooms. Add to onion and carrots, cook gently 2–3 minutes; remove and keep hot. **3.** Melt remaining 1 oz. butter in the pan, stir in flour and add tomatoes and liquid. Stir and cook until thickened. **4.** Drain tripe, put a layer into a buttered casserole dish, cover with one-third of sauce, then all the vegetables, followed by a layer of sauce and breadcrumbs. **5.** Add remaining tripe, remainder of sauce, and sprinkle with breadcrumbs. Dot with butter and bake in a hot oven mark 8 (450° F.) for 20 minutes or until golden brown.

Gypsy Pie

(Serves 4–6)

(From Miss R. Lock, Cirencester, Glos.)

---

1 small rabbit	salt and pepper
1 lb. beef steak	nutmeg
¼ lb. cooked ham or	stock
pork sausages	½ lb. rough puff pastry
1 teaspoon chopped parsley	

---

1. Soak rabbit in cold salted water 1½ hours. Wipe dry and joint. **2.** Finely chop ham (or skin sausages) and make meat into round balls with floured hands. **3.** Cut steak into small pieces. **4.** Arrange rabbit, ham, or meat balls and steak in pie dish, sprinkle with parsley, grated nutmeg, pepper, and salt to taste. Add stock and cover with pastry. **5.** Bake at mark 7 (425° F.) for approximately 25–30 minutes or until pastry is well risen and golden, then reduce heat to mark 4 (350° F.) and cook for a further 1–1½ hours or until meat is tender. When pastry has browned sufficiently, cover with kitchen foil to prevent over-browning.

Beefburger Nests

4 frozen beefburgers
1 lb. mashed potatoes
2 oz. grated cheese

4 eggs
salt and pepper

1. Put beefburgers on oven-proof dish. **2.** Add grated cheese to mashed potato and smooth over each beefburger. **3.** Scoop a deep well and break an egg into each one. Season lightly. **4.** Bake in oven mark 6 (400° F.) for about 20 minutes.

Salmon Pie

(Serves 6)

(From Mrs. E. Hurlock, Plumstead, London, who always cooks it for family gatherings on Good Friday)

8 oz. shortcrust pastry
2 large onions (sliced)
2 large potatoes (diced)
1 small packet peas
1 green pepper (chopped)
1 small tin tomato purée
1 small tin tomatoes
1 teaspoon chives (chopped)
½ teaspoon thyme
½ teaspoon paprika
1 small cauliflower
1 lb. tin pink salmon
cooking oil
salt and pepper to taste
¼ pint water
2 small cloves chopped garlic
 or garlic salt (optional)

1. Boil cauliflower and set aside to cool. **2.** Fry onions in cooking oil in large pan. Add garlic if liked. When brown, add ¼ pint of cold water and simmer 5 minutes. **3.** Add potatoes, peas, peppers, and chives and simmer for 10 minutes. **4.** Cut up tomatoes and add them with purée. Add thyme, paprika, salt, and pepper, 2 teaspoons cooking oil, and simmer for further 20 minutes. **5.** Add ¼ pint water and put sauce aside till cold. **6.** Set oven to mark 6 (400° F.). **7.** Thinly line 9½ × 3-inch deep pie tin with half pastry. **8.** Lay segments of cauliflower at bottom and pour sauce over. **9.** Flake salmon, lay on top, and cover with rest of pastry. **10.** Trim, brush with milk, and bake at mark 6 (400° F.) for 15–20 minutes, lowering heat to mark 4 (350° F.), until lightly browned. Cool before serving.

Liver Country Style (Serves 4)

4 rashers streaky bacon
1 lb. lambs' liver
2 oz. butter
4 oz. mushrooms (sliced)
3–4 medium onions (peeled
  and sliced)

1½ oz. plain flour
¾ pint stock
seasoning
juice ½ lemon

1. Chop bacon, fry until crisp and remove from pan. **2.** Brown liver in bacon fat and arrange in base of casserole. **3.** Lightly fry mushrooms in 1 oz. butter, remove from pan and keep on one side. **4.** Put onions in pan, fry gently until soft but not browned and remove. **5.** Add remaining 1 oz. butter to pan, stir in flour, then gradually stir in stock, seasoning to taste. **6.** When boiling add cooked bacon and onions and pour over liver. **7.** Cover and bake for 40 minutes at mark 3 (325° F.). Add mushrooms, cover, and bake further 20–30 minutes. Add lemon juice, adjust seasoning, and serve.

Plate Steak and Kidney Pie

(Serves 4–6)

14 oz. puff pastry
1 lb. stewing beef (cooked and diced)
6 oz. ox kidney (cooked and diced)

½ oz. butter
½ oz. flour
½ pint stock
milk for glazing
seasoning

1. Roll out half pastry to cover 8-inch oven-proof plate.
2. Place diced meat and kidney on pastry to within 1 inch of edge. 3. Melt butter in pan, stir in flour, and cook gently until brown, taking care not to burn. Stir in stock gradually and cook until thickened. Season to taste and pour over meats. 4. Cover with remaining pastry, rolled to fit size of plate. Seal edges, flake by cutting with back of knife and press into flutes. 5. Stand pie on baking tray and bake at mark 7 (425° F.) for 25–30 minutes.

Tattee 'Oggie

(Serves 4)

(From Mrs. Margaret Radford, Stretford, Lancs., who describes this as her own variation of one of the many versions of Cornish Pasty)

---

1 lb. shortcrust pastry (well seasoned)
½ lb. prime minced beef (rump, flank, or chuck)
¼ lb. lambs' liver
2 large potatoes

1 medium-sized swede
1 large onion
2 oz. butter
pepper and salt
chopped parsley (if desired)

---

1. Prepare pastry night before and store in cool part of fridge. Allow to warm to room temperature before use. **2.** Wash liver and cut into very small dice. **3.** Peel and wash potatoes and swede and cut into large chunks, then chop again to form thin slivers. (Ensure that swede is a little finer than potato as it takes longer to cook.) Chop onion finely. **4.** Place meat, liver, and vegetables in basin, season well and mix together thoroughly. **5.** Divide pastry into four, mould each piece into a ball, and roll out to size of large dinner plate. Place a quarter of the filling to cover half of the pastry and place a knob of butter on top. Moisten edges of pastry, fold over flap and crimp both ends firmly to seal. Repeat with remaining rounds. Place pasties on well-greased paper on baking sheet, brush with light eggwash or milk. **6.** Put in centre of a preheated oven mark 7 (425° F.) for 30 minutes, then turn down to mark 4 (350° F.) for approximately 45 minutes. If browning too quickly, cover with greaseproof paper. To check whether fully cooked, a knife inserted in the centre should cut through ingredients easily. Can be served hot or cold with salad. An excellent 'meal for family picnics'.

Braised Hearts

(Serves 4)

4 lambs' or sheeps' hearts
¼ lb. sausagemeat
pinch thyme
pinch nutmeg
pinch salt

1 teaspoon chopped parsley
2 oz. fresh white breadcrumbs
½ pint stock
2 oz. butter

1. Wash hearts well, cutting off all fat, gristle, and blood vessels. Cut through the centre divisions to make a cavity and soak in cold water for 30 minutes to remove all blood. **2.** Mix together sausagemeat, herbs, breadcrumbs, parsley, and a little stock. **3.** Fill each heart with stuffing, put into a casserole, dot with butter, and pour in remaining stock. **4.** Cover and cook on centre shelf of oven at mark 3 (325° F.) for 1½ hours. Baste well; return casserole without lid to oven and bake for further 30–45 minutes or until tender.

Cod in Cider

(Serves 4)

1 lb. cod fillet
8 mushrooms
2 large tomatoes (halved)
¼–½ pint cider

1 oz. butter or margarine
1 oz. plain flour
2 oz. grated cheese
salt and pepper

1. Cut cod in four and arrange in greased oven-proof dish with mushrooms and tomatoes. Pour in cider and season with salt and pepper. **2.** Bake at mark 5 (375° F.) for about 20 minutes. **3.** Add flour to melted butter and cook for a few minutes. Add liquid from fish with water if necessary to make ½ pint, bring to boil and cook for 2–3 minutes, stirring continuously. **4.** Pour over fish, sprinkle with grated cheese, and brown under hot grill.

Shepherd's Pie with Marrow

(Serves 2)

(From Miss Y. Tulinski, Leicester)

---

1 large marrow	1 lb. potatoes
½ lb. minced beef	milk and margarine for
1 onion (peeled and chopped)	creaming potatoes
1½ oz. fat	

---

1. Boil potatoes and mash with margarine, adding milk to taste. **2.** Heat the fat and fry onion and mince until brown. **3.** Preset oven to about mark 5 (375° F.). **4.** Meanwhile cut marrow in half and remove ends. Hollow out, removing pith and peeling off outer skin, leaving two cylinders of marrow. Cook for about 20 minutes in boiling water. **5.** Remove marrow from saucepan and place both halves on oven-proof dish. Spoon mince and onion into marrow and press down firmly. Spread mashed potato on top to fill and draw fork across top to give lined effect. **6.** Place dish in oven until potato is browned. Arrange halved, grilled tomatoes round each marrow portion for added colour. Serve one marrow half to each person.

Stuffed Breast of Lamb

(Serves 4)

1 breast of lamb
1 medium onion
1 small baking apple
½ oz. margarine (melted)
½ lb. sausagemeat

1 oz. fresh white breadcrumbs
pinch mixed herbs
1 teaspoon finely chopped
 parsley
little stock to bind if needed

1. Carefully cut out small bones from lamb. 2. Peel and chop onion and apple, add to melted margarine and fry gently until onion is soft but not brown. 3. Add sausagemeat and stir over low heat for 5 minutes. 4. Take off heat, stir in breadcrumbs, herbs, parsley, and seasoning to taste, adding stock if necessary. 5. Spread stuffing evenly over meat. Roll up neatly but not tightly and secure with string. 6. Roast for about 1½ hours at mark 3 (325° F.). Serve hot or cold.

Southern Fish Bake (Serves 4)

(From Mrs. R. Evans, Llandrillo, Corwen, Merioneth)

4 cod fillets
2 oz. butter
1 teaspoon chopped parsley

1 small chopped onion
1 grapefruit
2 oz. mushrooms (sliced)

1. Mix ⅔ parsley and onion with butter and grated rind of grapefruit. Place fish in shallow casserole, spread mixture over, then sprinkle with remaining parsley and onion and seasoning. **2.** Add mushrooms and juice of half the grapefruit. **3.** Place segments of remaining half grapefruit on top and cover. **4.** Bake at mark 5 (375° F.) for 30 minutes.

Toad-in-the-Hole (Serves 6)

¼ lb. plain flour
pinch salt
1 standard egg

½ pink milk
1 tablespoon butter (melted)
1 lb. pork sausages

1. Sift flour and salt together, add egg, ¼ pint milk, and butter, beating well. Stir in remaining milk. **2.** Arrange sausages in 10 × 12-inch baking tin and bake at mark 7 (425° F.) for 10 minutes. **3.** Remove from oven and quickly pour batter over; return to oven at mark 6 (400° F.) for a further 40–50 minutes until well-risen, set and browned.

Creole Rabbit Pie

(Serves 4–6)

(From Mrs. Eva Taylor, North Cotes' Grimsby, Lincs.)

---

6 oz. rough puff or flaky pastry
1 rabbit
2 oz. minced bacon
2 cooking apples (peeled and sliced)
1 onion (peeled and sliced)
2 tablespoons flour
1 dessertspoon curry powder
salt and pepper
pinch mixed herbs
1 dessertspoon chopped parsley
2 cloves
pinch mixed spice
½ pint stock
1 teaspoon Worcester sauce
1 dessertspoon lemon juice

---

1. Wash rabbit and cut into portions. Soak ½ hour in salted water. **2.** Place in saucepan and cover with hot water. Bring to boiling point, add salt, cloves, spice, and herbs. Simmer gently 1½ hours and remove to cool. **3.** Roll rabbit in flour mixed with curry powder. Place in bottom of greased pie dish, cover with layers of onion and apple. Top with minced bacon and chopped parsley and pour over stock and lemon juice. **4.** Roll pastry to ¼-inch thickness. Cover pie with pastry, trim edges, decorate if desired, and glaze with milk. **5.** Bake in hot oven mark 8 (450° F.) for 10 minutes, reduce heat to moderate mark 5 (375° F.) and cook for further 40–50 minutes.

Cheese Baked Potatoes

4 medium-sized potatoes
2 tablespoons milk
4 oz. grated Cheddar cheese

1 tablespoon chopped
parsley
salt and pepper

1. Wash potatoes and prick with fork. **2.** Bake at mark 4 (350° F.) for 1¼–1½ hours or until cooked. **3.** Cut potatoes in half, scoop out centre, and mash with fork. Beat in milk, grated cheese, chopped parsley, and season to taste. **4.** Return mixture to potato shells, reheat for a few minutes.

Shrimp Flan

(From Mrs. B. Hirst, Wath-on-Dearne, Yorks.)

Pastry:
4 oz. plain flour
2 oz. margarine
2 oz. white cheese (grated)
1 small egg to mix
pinch salt

Filling:
4 oz. shrimps (fresh, frozen or tinned)
2 eggs
5 oz. carton plain yoghurt
3 oz. packet cream cheese
1 teaspoon parsley (chopped)
salt and pepper

1. Mix flour and salt together, rub in fat and grated cheese and add beaten egg to make a stiff dough. **2.** Roll out pastry and line a 7-inch flan dish; prick well and bake blind at mark 6 (400° F.) for 15 minutes. **3.** Beat eggs, add yoghurt, cream cheese, salt and pepper, and chopped parsley and mix well. **4.** When cooked, cool flan case slightly, line with well-drained shrimps and pour filling on top. **5.** Bake on middle shelf of oven at mark 6 (400° F.) for about 30 minutes. Serve with cucumber salad.

Russian Fish Pie

(Serves 4)

7 oz. puff pastry
6–8 oz. cooked white fish
¼ pint thick white sauce

1 teaspoon chopped parsley
1 or 2 hard-boiled eggs
salt and pepper

1. Roll out pastry into square and trim edges. **2.** Flake fish and mix with sauce and parsley, seasoning to taste. **3.** Put filling in centre of pastry. Bring four corners to centre. Carefully arrange slices of egg on filling. **4.** Cut four leaves out of pastry trimmings; brush pastry with milk and decorate with leaves. **5.** Bake at mark 7 (425° F.) for approximately 30 minutes, or until well risen and golden brown.

Roasted Fruity Lamb (Serves 4)

(From Mrs. C. Coleman, Buckden, Huntingdon)

1½–2 lb. boned leg of lamb
Stuffing:
1 small onion (finely chopped)
1 oz. roasted, salted peanuts
  (crushed)
1 tablespoon parsley
  (chopped)

1 small tin apricot halves
3 oz. fresh breadcrumbs
½ teaspoon lemon (or
  orange) juice
1 beaten egg
½ oz. butter or margarine
pepper to season

1. Wash lamb in cold water and remove excess fat. **2.** Mix onion, nuts, and parsley in bowl. Drain apricots, chop in pieces, and add to mixture with breadcrumbs, fruit juice, and seasoning. Bind with beaten egg. **3.** Place stuffing into meat cavity and secure with string. Put in casserole dish, dot with butter or margarine, and cover. **4.** Roast for 1 hour at mark 5 (375° F.). Remove casserole lid and continue roasting for further 30 minutes.

Make the Money go Round

It's amazing what you can do to stretch a family food budget when you use a bit of ingenuity. And you'll find that the recipes in this section are mostly easy on time and effort too.

Bacon Extravaganza (Serves 2–3)

(From Miss J. Austin, Walney Island, Barrow-in-Furness, Lancs.

---

6 rashers back bacon (green
  or salted) or bacon roll
6 beef sausages
2 oz. sausagemeat
4 large potatoes
1 jar cloves
1 large Spanish onion
1 packet sage and onion
  stuffing

1 bunch thyme (or generous
  pinch dried thyme)
1 jar olives (stuffed or pitted)
1 beef stock cube
salt and cayenne pepper
2 large tomatoes
butter
pinch sweet basil (dried)
6 small wooden skewers

---

1. Set oven at mark 7 (425° F.). **2.** Empty packet of stuffing into
mixing bowl and add sausagemeat. Mix well and add finely
chopped onion, salt, and pepper. Dissolve stock cube in ⅔ pint
water and pour into stuffing. Mix and leave to stand. **3.** Scrub
potatoes clean and thread each one on to a metal skewer
coated with butter. Stick each potato with cloves, and put on
metal tray. Place in oven and leave to cook for 15 minutes.
4. Grease large casserole dish with butter. Trim bacon and on
each slice spread a layer of stuffing. **5.** Take a sausage and roll
bacon round it, securing with a wooden skewer. Put one olive
at each end of bacon roll. Repeat six times. **6.** Place sausage
and bacon rolls in casserole dish, add knob of butter and pinch
of salt and cayenne pepper. Wash and chop herbs and
sprinkle over. **7.** Wash tomatoes and zig-zag cut in half,
sprinkle with sweet basil and arrange round casserole dish.
Bake for 45 minutes—1 hour altogether with potatoes.

Banana Doolittle

(Serves 4)

(From Mrs. J. Stroud, Lee, London)

½ lb. pork chipolata sausages
4 tomatoes (peeled and
  sliced)
4 bananas

1 medium onion (peeled and
  sliced)
1 teaspoon brown sugar
¼ pint water
pepper and salt

1. Lay sausages in bottom of greased casserole and cover with layer of sliced tomatoes and onions. **2.** Slice bananas lengthways and arrange on top. **3.** Pour water over, seasoned with pepper, salt, and sugar. **4.** Cook 1 hour in oven at mark 4 (350° F.).

Cheesy Leek Flan (Serves 4)

8-inch baked shortcrust
  pastry case
1 oz. butter
1 oz. plain flour
1 lb. leeks
½ pint milk

seasoning
1 level teaspoon mustard
  (made)
4 oz. Cheddar cheese
  (grated)

1. Cut leeks into ¼-inch thick rings and wash well. Melt ½ oz. butter in pan and add leeks; cover pan and cook gently for 2–3 minutes. **2.** Melt remaining butter in saucepan and stir in flour. Add milk, stirring well, and cook well until sauce is smooth and thick. Stir in mustard and 3 oz. grated cheese and season to taste. **3.** Spoon leeks into baked, hot, flan case, top with sauce and sprinkle with remaining cheese. Bake in oven at mark 6 (400° F.) for 15 minutes.

Golden Bake

(Serves 4–6)

(From Mrs. D. Bell, Eastleigh, Hants.)

---

4 oz. grated cheese
8 oz. cooked chicken or ham
1 onion
1 tablespoon chopped
  parsley (optional)

2 oz. white breadcrumbs
2 eggs
$\frac{1}{4}$ pint milk
$\frac{1}{4}$ pint single cream
salt and pepper

---

1. Mince meat and onion finely; add parsley, breadcrumbs and cheese and season. **2.** Separate eggs; beat together yolks with milk and cream and stir into meat mixture. Fold in stiffly beaten egg whites. **3.** Turn into greased oven-proof dish and bake in moderate oven mark 5 (375° F.) for 40–50 minutes, until risen and golden brown.

Cheese Whispers

(From Mrs. J. S. Hopper, Frodsham, Cheshire, who says they make impressive cocktail savouries or a good supper dish with bacon)

½ packet instant mashed
  potato
2 oz. butter
2 oz. plain flour

1 egg
4 oz. Gruyère cheese
salt and pepper

1. Prepare potato following instructions but using only half stated amount of water. Mix in butter and flour. **2.** Beat egg, grate cheese, and add to mixture with seasoning. **3.** Place in teaspoonfuls on greased baking sheet, leaving ½-inch spaces between each. Bake at mark 7 (425° F.) for 15 minutes or until golden brown.

Cowboy Lunch

(Serves 4)

(From Mrs. Alison Hills, Bourne, Lincs.)

---

6 oz. corned beef
1 small tin baked beans
 (curried if liked)
8 oz. self-raising flour

5 oz. lard
½ teaspoon salt
cold water (about ¼ pint)

---

1. Chop corned beef into small cubes and mix well with beans in basin, seasoning to taste. **2.** In another basin mix flour and salt. Cut lard into very small pieces and rub into flour. Mix to a stiff paste with cold water. **3.** Turn on to floured board and roll out to oblong shape. Spread corned beef and beans along the centre, wet edges well with milk, fold over and seal edges. Prick over top slightly and brush with a little milk. **4.** Put on baking sheet and bake in a hot oven mark 7 (425° F.) for about 30–45 minutes.

Giblet Pie

(Serves 4)

(From Mrs. M. Aunger, Colne, Lancs.)

Giblets from chicken, duck, goose or turkey*
1 oz. suet
1 lb. onions
4 oz. breadcrumbs
½ teaspoon sage
6 oz. shortcrust pastry
salt and pepper

1. Chop giblets except gizzard, wash in cold water, and cook in salted water until tender. **2.** Chop and boil onion until tender, strain and add breadcrumbs, suet, sage, and seasoning. **3.** Place giblets in an 8-inch pie plate and cover with onion forcemeat. **4.** Roll out pastry, cover pie plate and brush with beaten egg. **5.** Bake in moderate oven mark 5 (375° F.) for 30 minutes, until golden brown.

* Editor's note. As quantity by weight varies with size of bird it may be necessary to use two sets of giblets. Remember to discard gizzard after cooking.

Baked Dumpling Surprise

(Serves 4)

(From Mrs. S. Courteney, Westcliff-on-Sea, Essex)

½ lb. self-raising flour
¼ lb. suet
pinch salt
water to mix

8 lambs' kidneys
8 rashers streaky bacon
  (trimmed)
melted fat

---

1. Mix flour, suet, salt, and water to stiff dough. Roll out and divide into eight dumplings. **2.** Skin and core lambs' kidneys, wrap each one in streaky bacon rasher and encase completely in one portion of dough. **3.** Bake in a little hot fat at mark 6 (400° F.) for 30 minutes or until dumplings are crisp and brown. Garnish if liked with baked tomatoes.

Kipper Flan

(Serves 2–4)

7-inch unbaked pastry flan
  case
1 small packet kipper fillets
Cheese sauce:
1 oz. butter or margarine
1 oz. plain flour
½ pint milk

1 egg yolk
1 teaspoon made mustard
2 oz. grated Cheddar cheese
pepper
1 dessertspoon chopped
  parsley

1. Arrange kipper fillets in flan case. **2.** Prepare cheese sauce
and stir in parsley. Pour over flan. **3.** Bake at mark 5 (375° F.) for
approximately 30 minutes, or until golden brown.

Horseshoe Surprise

(Serves 4)

(From Mrs. Mavis Oliver, Flint, Wales)

Scone Mix:
1 oz. butter
4 oz. self-raising flour
2 oz. grated mature
  Cheddar cheese
salt and pepper
a little milk
Topping:
1 oz. grated cheese

Filling:
1 small onion (peeled and
  chopped)
1 oz. butter
7½ oz. can salmon or tuna
  (drained and flaked)
1 oz. grated mature Cheddar
  cheese
1 level dessertspoon
  chopped parsley

1. Rub butter into flour, add cheese and seasoning, and bind with milk. Roll out to make 10×5½-inch rectangle. **2.** Cook onion in butter and mix in salmon or tuna, 1 oz. cheese, and parsley. **3.** Pile mixture lengthways along scone, wet edges and roll up, bending into horseshoe shape. **4.** Place on greased baking sheet. Make a few slits in top and sprinkle on remaining cheese. **5.** Bake in a fairly hot oven mark 6 (400° F.) for approximately 30 minutes. Serve hot.

Lattice Loaf

(Serves 2)

7-oz. tin luncheon meat
7 oz. puff pastry

½ packet sage and onion
    stuffing (scant)

1. Roll out pastry into rectangle approximately 10×8 inches. Cut slanting strips towards the centre, 2 inches long by 1 inch wide, down two long edges of pastry. **2.** Make up stuffing as directed. **3.** Cut meat into four even slices, arrange two slices to form oblong down centre of pastry, spread with half stuffing, then cover with remaining meat and stuffing. **4.** Plait strips of pastry over meat, sealing ends neatly, and brush with milk. **5.** Bake at mark 7 (425° F.) for 15 minutes, then reduce heat to mark 5 (375° F.) for further 15 minutes. Serve hot or cold.

Mock Roast

(Serves 4–6)

(From Mrs. I. Hitchon, St. Peters, Broadstairs, Kent)

---

1 lb. sausagemeat
4–6 oz. left-over cooked meat
(minced)
1 small onion (grated)
1 teaspoon mixed dried herbs
2 oz. breadcrumbs
1 egg
melted dripping

Coating cream:
1 dessertspoon flour
1 dessertspoon gravy powder
½ teaspoon dry mustard

(blend to thick cream with
cold water)

---

1. Mix sausagemeat together with cooked meat, onion, herbs, and breadcrumbs and bind with beaten egg. **2.** Mould to joint shape with floured hands and place in baking tin with melted dripping. Brush over with coating cream. **3.** Place in moderate oven mark 5 (375° F.) for 20 minutes. **4.** Baste with fat, then repeat with coating cream and repeat at intervals until joint is done, approximately 1 hour. Serve hot with vegetables in season or cold with salad.

Macaroni Slices

(Serves 4–6)

(From Mrs. E. Websdale, Bloxham, Banbury, Oxon.)

---

4 oz. macaroni
3 oz. lentils
4 oz. breadcrumbs
1 small onion or 2 shallots
  (peeled and chopped)

1 oz. margarine or butter
seasoning to taste
grated cheese

---

1. Soak lentils overnight. **3.** Cook lentils and macaroni (separately) until soft. Mash them together and work in breadcrumbs. **3.** Fry chopped onion in margarine or butter and when lightly coloured add to mixture, with any fat not absorbed by the onion. Season generously. **4.** Grease loaf-shaped cake tin and press in mixture. Cover with greased paper and bake in moderate oven mark 4 (350° F.) for 1 hour. **5.** When cold turn out, cut into slices, and divide into fingers. Sprinkle thickly with grated cheese and brown in oven or under grill. If liked, serve with tomato or onion sauce.

Monday Bake

(Serves 6)

(From Mrs. B. Knowles, Richmond, Yorks.)

12 oz. cooked cold meat
1 small cabbage
2 tablespoons milk
1 lb. cooking apples
½ oz. plain flour

2 lb. potatoes
2½ oz. margarine
1 oz. sugar
salt, pepper, nutmeg

1. Peel and boil potatoes, prepare and cook cabbage. 2. Cut meat into short strips. 3. Cream cooked potatoes with 1 oz. margarine and a little milk, seasoning with salt and pepper and a little nutmeg. 4. Drain and coarsely chop cabbage and mix in ½ oz. margarine. 5. Peel, core, and slice apples. Cook with 1 oz. sugar in very little water until soft. 6. Melt 1 oz. margarine in pan, blend in ½ oz. flour, add 2 tablespoons water, and stir until smooth. Add cooked apple and bring to the boil. Cook, stirring for 2 minutes. 7. Mix in cabbage. 8. Line bottom of a casserole with creamed potato, put meat in centre and cover with apple and cabbage mixture. 9. Heat at mark 4 (350° F.) for about 30 minutes.

Savoury Mince Bake (Serves 2)

8 oz. shortcrust pastry
1 can minced beef with
  onions

3 tomatoes (skinned and
  sliced)
¾ lb. creamed potatoes

1. Roll out pastry and line 8-inch flan ring. **2.** Spread mince evenly over base of pastry and arrange tomatoes on top.
3. Pipe or fork creamed potatoes over top to completely cover.
4. Bake at mark 6 (400° F.) for 20–25 minutes.

Onions Stuffed with Liver and Bacon

(Serves 4)

4 large onions (skinned)
¼ lb. lambs' liver (chopped)
¼ lb. lean bacon (chopped)

seasoning
1 oz. butter

1. Cook onions in boiling salted water for 30 minutes and drain.
2. Cut a slice off top of each and carefully remove centres, leaving ¾-inch-thick onion shells. 3. Mix together liver and bacon, season to taste and spoon into onion shells. 4. Top each onion with knob of butter and stand in ovenproof dish; add 5 tablespoons of water. 5. Bake uncovered at mark 5 (375° F.) for about 45 minutes, until tender. Baste frequently.

Pensioner's Casserole (Serves 2)

(From Miss E. Atkin, Sketty, Swansea, who rightly describes this as a nourishing and helpful dish)

---

1 small cabbage
4 oz. rice
bacon bones
½ lb. bacon pieces

2 oz. sultanas
large pinch mixed herbs
1 bay leaf
salt and pepper

---

1. Wash rice in cold water and put into casserole. Add washed bacon bones, the leanest pieces of bacon cut into strips, shredded cabbage heart, and washed sultanas. **2.** Pour on 1 pint boiling water, cover with well-fitting lid and place in moderate oven mark 4 (350° F.) for 1 hour, or until rice and cabbage are quite tender. (If preferred, cook in pan over low heat, simmering until contents are tender.) Add extra water or stock if needed: when cooked, ingredients should be moist, but not wet like soup. Serve on slices of toast or with toast fingers.

Quick Salmon Pie

(Serves 4–6)

(From Mrs. E. Shreeve, Frinton-on-Sea, Essex)

1 beaten egg
3 cups instant mashed
  potato, prepared and cooled
2 cups frozen or tinned peas
1 large tin pink salmon
2 eggs (unbeaten)
1 tablespoon lemon juice

10-oz. tin celery soup
¼ cup salad cream
2 green onions (chopped)
4 large slices bread
  (crumbled)
salt and pepper to taste

1. Beat one egg into potato and spread in bottom and up sides of buttered 9-inch-square baking tin. Sprinkle with peas. **2.** Remove skin from salmon and empty salmon and juice into a food mixer. Add eggs, lemon juice, soup, salad cream, onions, and blend until well mixed. **3.** Add crumbs, salt and pepper and spoon mixture over peas. **4.** Bake at mark 4 (350° F.) for 40–50 minutes, or until set. Cool slightly and serve with a green salad.

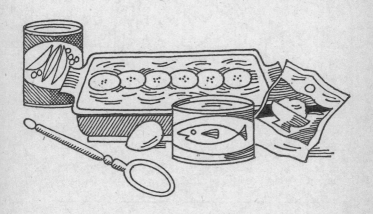

Sweet Spiced Herrings

(Serves 2)

¼ pint vinegar
¼ pint water
1 bay leaf
1 oz. brown sugar
4 cloves stuck in medium
  onion

few peppercorns
1 level teaspoon salt
4 herring fillets

1. Put all ingredients except herring into saucepan and boil together for 5 minutes. **2.** Sprinkle fillets with salt and pepper and roll up, skin side outside, from head to tail. Pack into baking dish arranging with 'tails in the air'. **3.** Top with buttered greaseproof paper and bake at mark 4 (350° F.) for 30 minutes.

Mushroom and Celery Pie

(Serves 4)

(From Mr. E. J. Page, St. Albans, Herts.—our only male prize-winner)

½ lb. mushrooms
1 medium-size head of celery
4 rashers fat bacon
6 oz. shortcrust pastry

salt, pepper, lemon juice
a little butter
a little milk and water

---

1. Skin mushrooms and remove stalks. Sprinkle undersides with salt; allow to stand until salt dissolves, then wipe dry. Cut into even medium-size pieces. **2.** Wash celery and cut into even moderate-size pieces. **3.** Fill a pie dish with alternate layers of bacon, mushrooms, and celery, sprinkling each layer with salt, pepper, and a few drops of lemon juice. Add about 2 tablespoons of milk and water. Dot top with butter and cover whole with pastry. **4.** Bake in fairly hot oven mark 6 (400° F.) for 10 minutes, then cover with sheet of greaseproof paper. Finish baking in moderate oven mark 4 (350° F.) for another 20–30 minutes. Serve hot.

Scotch Eggs

(Serves 3)

3 hard-boiled eggs (standard) fresh brown breadcrumbs
½ lb. sausagemeat   for coating
beaten egg

1. Shell eggs, divide sausagemeat into three equal pieces, and carefully mould round each egg. **2.** Brush well with egg and coat with breadcrumbs. **3.** Place on well-greased tray and bake 20–25 minutes at mark 5 (375° F.). Serve hot or cold.

Stuffed Tomatoes

(Serves 4)

4 large tomatoes
7-oz. can tuna

seasoning
½ oz. butter

1. Cut tops off tomatoes and keep to one side. Scoop out tomato centres into basin, discarding any hard pieces. **2.** Drain and flake tuna and mix well with tomato in basin. Season to taste. **3.** Pile tuna filling generously into tomatoes and dot with butter. Place on greased ovenproof dish with any remaining filling and tomato tops. **4.** Bake at mark 6 (400° F.) for 15 minutes. Remove from oven and transfer tomatoes to warm serving dish, spooning over any extra filling and replacing tomato tops. Serve with rice.

Sage and Onion Pudding
(Serves 4–6)

(From Miss B. Bailey, Lancing, Sussex, who calls it 'a good extra filler for a chilly day and an unusual change from Yorkshire pudding')

---

2 teaspoons sage
2 oz. chopped suet
2 oz. fine oatmeal
seasoning to taste
milk for mixing

5 oz. breadcrumbs
2½ tablespoons chopped
  onions
small dash Worcester sauce

---

1. Mix all ingredients together thoroughly, adding just enough milk to give soft consistency. **2.** Turn into well-greased tin and bake in pre-heated moderate oven mark 4 (350° F.) for 1 hour. Cut into generous squares and serve with any meat and gravy.

Shopping Wisely

You probably received this book as part of our celebrations to mark the opening of a new Co-op food store. If so you will have now seen for yourself the benefits that shopping at *your* Co-op can bring: good food, low prices *and a share of the profits too.*

In **Baking Your Cake & Eating It** you'll find a whole series of useful ideas on how to make your money go further when it comes to cooking in the oven. Most of the recipes have been sent in by housewives working to a set budget for the family's food.

In these next few pages you'll find some further advice on making the most of the housekeeping. Just one of the many ways in which the Co-op cuts the cost of family shopping.

Consumer Service— Co-op were first in the field

Let us in imagination board H. G. Wells's Time Machine and go back to 1844.

To a Lancashire town, Rochdale, perched on the lower slopes of the Pennines.

Life was hard in those days, much harsher than it is now. The cost of living then as now was an acute problem and it was aggravated by shoddy goods, short weight and adulteration of food.

Twenty-eight men of Rochdale did more than complain. They acted. They clubbed together a few coppers a week. They bought a few basic foods from a reputable merchant, supplied themselves at fair prices and at the end of a few months paid back the "profit" as a dividend of so much in the pound of each member's purchases.

The Biggest

They had "invented" the consumers' co-operative movement, better known as the Co-op. Their idea was copied all over the country and in scores of other countries. One hundred and thirty years later the consumers' co-op has become the biggest retailer in Britain.

Today, while some societies still pay a cash dividend, your share of the profits is generally in the form of dividend stamps which you can exchange for goods or invest in your member's share account with your society.

The "discovery" of the consumer by Government and the Press has taken a long time. Better late than never. But **your** Co-op pioneered the road —and is still the most widespread and powerful consumer guardian at the point where it really matters—in the shops.

How to be a price-wise housewife by Marion Giordan

formerly editor of "Insight", the Housewife's Trust's magazine, and well-known broadcaster and writer on consumer affairs.

PRICES HAVE been rising at a frightening rate. We get a lot of vague advice about "value for money" and "shopping around", but what does it really mean? How can we beat the price-rise system when all around us prices are going up? Here are some practical points to help you in your shopping at a time when money is tight, there are a lot of demands on it, and inflation is pushing prices up.

First of all, what is "value for money"? We are always being urged to look out for it but it means different things to different people. Basically, it means value for money to you. It depends on your own personal tastes, the money you've got to spend, the number of people in the family and the sort of things they like.

It depends on the time you've got available for shopping, where you live and how far you are from the shops. It depends on whether you've got a car or not, and whether you are strong enough to carry home great loads of shopping or whether you've got to wait for the weekend to use the car.

Most women want to do the best for their families with the money that's available: their families don't want to see them exhausted by struggling round the shops chasing bargains—which is what "shopping around" usually comes to. Not everyone has the strength or the energy and time to shop around, so you have to work out which means most to you—time, low prices, or effort.

But having sorted that out in your own mind, you can be your own best friend and try some practical advice to help you to be a cautious, well-informed shopper. Because that's the only way, in the confusing and fast-changing situation that shopping is today, that a shopper can protect herself.

1. Take advantage of special low prices. Expensive doesn't necessarily mean best. When some lines are cut price, buy them and possibly stock up with them. Then watch the other prices in the store to make sure they haven't been put up to compensate for the low ones.

2. Shop at non-peak hours when there are fewer crowds, less bustle and it's easier to make a choice. Monday is the slackest day, rising to Friday and Saturday.

3. Read the label. A lot of useful information is there, including price and weight. Look at these to see how much you are getting for your money. Some packaging is deceptive: you might think you were buying a full pound until you look at the label and find it's really 12 ounces.

4. Look at the own-label products: Co-op stores have a big range. Own-label goods are often good value and cheaper than branded goods.

5. Look around. When the price of one item goes up (or its contents go down and the price remains the same) look at the competition. See if you can find another product like it, the same quantity, and at the lower price.

6. Fresh often means cheap, particularly when you buy fresh fruit and vegetables in season. Strawberries are at their best and cheapest for a few weeks in the summer; during the winter they are a luxury. Apples can be expensive from January to March, at a time when oranges might be cheaper. Oranges are better for you anyway because they are full of essential vitamin C—the anti-cold vitamin. In any case fresh fruit and vegetables can be cheaper than buying processed, depending on the time of year, so compare for value.

7. Expensive cuts of meat aren't the only form of protein. Look at cheap cuts—or special offers too. Long careful cooking makes cheap cuts an interesting meal. Remember that there are other, cheaper forms of protein—frozen chicken, tinned meat and fish, eggs, cheese, and milk.

8. Finally, don't go mad on buying the cheapest just for the sake of a low price. If your family doesn't like it or won't eat it, it's been an extravagance rather than a saving. If something costs a little more and you like it and will enjoy every bit of it, then the choice is yours.

The Co-op Seasonal Guide to Value for Money with Meat

	JAN	FEB	MAR	APR	MAY	JUN	JLY	AUG	SPT	OCT	NOV	DEC
BEEF	*	*	*	*	■	■	■	■	*	*	*	*
VEAL	■	■	■	■	■	■	■	■	■	■	■	■
PORK	*	*	*	*	■	■	■	■	*	*	*	*
ENG. LAMB	■	■	■	■	*	*	*	*	*	*	*	■
N. Z. LAMB	*	*	*	*	■	■	■	■	■	■	■	*
CHICKEN	*	*	*	*	*	■	■	■	■	■	*	*
TURKEY	*	*	*	*	*	*	*	*	*	*	*	*
DUCKLING	*	*	*	*	*	*	*	*	*	*	*	*
BACON	*	*	*	*	*	*	*	*	*	*	*	*
OFFAL	*	*	*	*	*	*	*	*	*	*	*	*

SYMBOL * BEST VALUE ■ GOOD VALUE

Co-op Bank
Sets the pace

WALK AROUND any town centre in Britain, from the great cities to the smallest country town.

Shops will be the main occupants of many of the streets. But prominent among them will be the banks. Sometimes two or three side by side or facing each other. Sometimes spread out more widely. But never for long out of your sight.

Once they did not mean much to most of us. Banks were for industry, commerce, business, the monetary affairs of large organisations. Not for us.

They still, of course, carry on their traditional business. But you, the consumer, are now the new and important client in the banking and credit scene.

It is all part of the consumer credit revolution. Banks, finance houses and credit card organisations are competing to lend you money, either as direct loans or in the form of credit facilities.

Personal loans, instant credit, credit cards, most of them usable at home and in many foreign countries. Hire purchase. Credit in many forms is now an essential part of the life style of the twentieth century consumer.

It is consumer credit, planned and budgeted within one's income, that enables millions of people to enjoy home and personal amenities they would otherwise have gone without.

But, as with all other goods and services; it has to be paid for and the charge is made in the form of interest.

The interest rate can be expressed in one of two ways, either as the flat rate or the true rate.

And the way in which it is expressed can make a big difference to what you are actually paying for your loan.

A flat rate of, say, 10 per cent, means that for the whole period of the loan you are paying 10 per cent on the original sum borrowed.

The amount outstanding falls with each periodic repayment. But flat rate interest is still 10 per cent on the original loan, not on the diminishing balance outstanding.

To calculate the true rate of interest you are paying, the 10 per cent should be expressed as a percentage of the diminishing balance after each repayment. It is a complicated exercise which not many of us would find easy to carry out.

Which is where the Co-operative Bank comes in.

It is the first bank in Britain to publicise the true annual rate of interest on its credit business.

The Co-operative Bank can also claim to be the Convenient Bank.

It has 40 full scale branches and is opening

others. In addition, through the co-operation of local societies, banking facilities are provided at more than 4,000 bank points in Co-op societies, many of which offer facilities on Saturdays. There may be one at your local Co-op. Ask next time you are out shopping.

Backing up the Co-operative Bank are combined assets of £223 millions. It is Britain's sixth largest bank—and growing fast.

The Co-op helps housewives with Freezers, Too

A deep freezer is fast becoming standard equipment in Britain's kitchens as more and more housewives invest in a home unit of their own.

For the freezer has more to offer than saving money, important though that may be.

Housewives with freezers spend less time preparing and buying foods—that means more time for their families. Then there's the convenience of one-stop shopping and having on hand a good stock of varied dishes for more exciting family eating or to cater for those unexpected guests. And fresh foods bought during seasonal gluts plus low price bulk packs means savings of the most direct kind.

To meet shoppers' needs in the home freezer era, Co-op freezer food centres are growing up fast. Already there are more Co-op centres than any others and all are designed to offer a comprehensive service to the housewife.

You can choose from a wide range of competitively priced cabinets the one that will meet your personal requirements. Trained staff are available who will assist and advise on all aspects of home freezers including helping to arrange credit agreements and insurance benefits.

Up to 300 bulk size food products are sold in a typical Co-op freezer food centre.

They range from specialities like chinese meals, Danish pastries and pizza to the more basic items such as fish fingers, beef burgers, vegetables and ice-cream, which you may already be buying in small packs two or three times a week. Now with the larger freezer packs you can save as much as a third on the price of these items.

It has been estimated that by the end of 1973 some two million families in Britain will own a home freezer.

Why not pay a visit to your local Co-op freezer food centre and learn for yourself the benefits which your family could obtain.

For the address of your nearest Co-op freezer food centre write to:

Mr. J. Chambers
Public Relations Department
Co-operative Wholesale Society Ltd
New Century House
Manchester M60 4ES

Give Them a Sweet Surprise

All these puddings are really mouth-watering
and as most of them use fresh fruit they can
be varied to suit both taste and season. They
include basic stand-bys and special-
occasion spectaculars.

Apple Almond Pie

(Serves 4–6)

(From Mrs. G. Osborn, Ashby, Scunthorpe, Lincs.)

1 lb. cooked apples or 3 cups apple pulp
9 oz. plain flour
6 oz. butter or substitute
1 egg yolk
4 tablespoons sour cream, single cream or plain yoghurt

2 oz. ground almonds
2 oz. sugar
2 tablespoons strawberry jam
1 egg white
water and sugar for glazing
¼ pint whipped double cream

1. Sieve flour and salt and rub in butter to consistency of breadcrumbs. Mix to a dough with egg yolk and cream or yoghurt. Knead and put aside in cool place for 30 minutes. **2.** Line 9-inch pie plate with half pastry, prick with fork, and bake for 10 minutes in hot oven mark 6 (400° F.). **3.** Mix ground almonds with sugar. **4.** Remove pastry from oven, spread with strawberry jam, and sprinkle with half almond and sugar mixture. **5.** Beat egg white until stiff and fold into stewed apple, spoon on to pie, sprinkle the rest of almonds and sugar over. **6.** Cover with remaining pastry, glaze, sprinkle with sugar, and make a few slits in pie top. **7.** Bake in hot oven mark 6 (400° F.) for approximately 30 minutes. When cool top with whipped double cream.

Apple Charlotte

1 lb. cooking apples
2 oz. sugar
juice and peel of $\frac{1}{2}$ lemon
1 oz. margarine

2 egg yolks
small white loaf
3 oz. butter or good quality
  margarine (melted)

1. Peel and core apples, cut into small pieces, and cook very gently. Sieve or liquidize, stir in sugar, lemon peel, and juice, 1 oz. margarine, and egg yolks. **2.** Remove crusts from loaf and cut bread into $\frac{1}{4}$-inch slices; cut two slices into rounds to fit base and top of 5–6-inch soufflé dish. Measure depth of dish and cut remaining bread into fingers of same length. Place round of bread into base of dish; dip each finger into melted butter and arrange closely together to line dish sides. **3.** Pour in apple mixture and cover with remaining round of bread. Bake at mark 4 (350° F.) for 1–1$\frac{1}{2}$ hours, or until bread is brown and crisp. Turn out and dredge with caster sugar.

Plum Wheels

(Serves 4)

(From Mrs. Gillian D. Nicholas, Chelmsley Wood, Birmingham, who says it makes an extra-special pudding much enjoyed by her family as a change from Christmas Pudding)

8 oz. shortcrust pastry
15-oz. tin red plums
4 oz. sultanas or mixed dried fruit

2 oz. sugar
2 oz. softened butter or margarine

1. Set oven at mark 6 (400° F.). **2.** Roll out pastry to oblong shape, approximately ⅜-inch thick. **3.** Strain tin of plums (saving syrup), stone and place in a basin. Add sultanas or mixed fruit and sugar, mixing well together. **4.** Spread softened butter carefully over pastry then spread plum mixture over, leaving about 1 inch uncovered around the edges. **5.** Roll pastry into Swiss Roll shape, cut slices of approximately 1 inch thick and place in a shallow casserole dish. **6.** Pour plum syrup over and bake in centre of oven until golden brown on top (about 30 minutes). Serve with cream, custard, or evaporated milk.

Short, Short Pastry

(From Mrs. E. Hollingworth, Whitestone, Exeter, Devon, who says, 'It breaks all pastry-making rules and is so easy to mix that even small children can do it. But it tastes very good!')

4 oz. margarine
1 oz. caster sugar

1 dessertspoon hot water
7 oz. self-raising flour

1. Warm bowl. **2.** Add hot water to fat and sugar in bowl and beat to a soft cream. **3.** Gradually work in flour with a fork. **4.** Knead pastry into ball. **5.** Leave in refrigerator for 30 minutes at least before using. Roll out on well-floured board.

Baked Alaska

(Serves 4)

7-inch sponge flan case
2 egg whites
4 oz. icing sugar

1 small can strawberries
 (strained)
small block strawberry ice
 cream

1. Whisk together egg whites and icing sugar into stiff peaks.
2. Place flan case on baking tray and cover base with straw-berries. 3. Place ice cream on top, then quickly spread meringue over whole, making sure there are no gaps. 4. Bake just a few minutes at mark 8 (450° F.) until meringue is golden. Serve immediately.

Honey Tart

(Serves 4)

(From Mrs. Flisher, Maidstone, Kent, who says it is the favourite sweet in her family)

Shortcrust pastry:
4 oz. plain flour
½ teaspoon salt
1 oz. margarine
1 oz. lard
cold water to mix

Filling:
4 oz. cream cheese
2 level tablespoons clear
  honey
2 oz. caster sugar
½ teaspoon cinnamon
2 standard eggs

---

1. Preheat oven to mark 5 (375° F.). **2.** Prepare pastry, roll out, and line shallow 7-inch square tin so that pastry comes half way up sides. **3.** Place cream cheese in bowl, add honey, caster sugar and cinnamon, beating until smooth. Beat eggs and gradually add to mixture, beating well all the time. **4.** Pour mixture in pastry case and sprinkle with a little cinnamon and caster sugar. **5.** Place tart in centre of oven and bake for 35 minutes. Remove from oven, cut into squares, remove from tin, and leave to cool on wire rack.

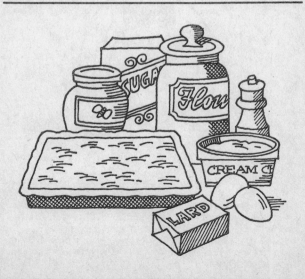

Baked Egg Custard

3 large eggs

1 pint milk

1 oz. caster sugar

grated nutmeg

1. Beat eggs and milk together, strain into 1½-pint oven-proof dish. Stir in sugar and sprinkle nutmeg lightly on top. **2.** Stand dish in roasting tin containing sufficient water to come halfway up sides of dish. Bake at mark 3 (325° F.) for ¾–1 hour or until firm.

Banana and Raisin Pie

(From Mrs. D. Ransome, Kings Lynn, Norfolk)   (Serves 4–6)

8-inch flan case
1 oz. cornflour
½ pint milk
1 oz. caster sugar
2 egg yolks (beaten)
½ oz. margarine

2 bananas (sliced)
1½ oz. raisins (chopped)
1 oz. flaked almonds
Meringue:
2 egg whites
2 oz. caster sugar

1. Bake flan case. **2.** Mix cornflour with little milk, bring remaining milk to boil. Pour over cornflour and mix well. Return to pan and cook for 3–4 minutes. **3.** Stir in sugar, egg yolks, and margarine, then add raisins, almonds, and sliced bananas. Pour into pastry case. **4.** Whisk egg whites until stiff, whisk in half sugar, fold in remainder of sugar, and pipe or pile over flan. **5.** Bake at mark 6 (400° F.) for about 15–20 minutes or until meringue is brown.

Caramel Rice

(Serves 4)

Rice filling:
2 oz. pudding rice
½ pint milk
½ oz. sugar
½ oz. butter
1 egg

Caramel:
3 oz. granulated sugar
¼ pint water (scant)

1. Put sugar and water into saucepan and heat slowly until sugar is dissolved; bring to boil and boil until golden brown. **2.** Pour caramel into soufflé dish or small cake tin. Protecting hands with thick cloth, revolve caramel round sides and base of mould until coated and set. **3.** Put washed rice and milk into saucepan and cook, stirring frequently, over low heat until rice is soft and mixture thickens. **4.** Stir in butter, sugar, and egg and pour into caramel-lined dish. Cover with greased grease-proof paper or foil. **5.** Stand in roasting tin containing hot water and bake approximately 45 minutes or until set at mark 3 (325° F.). Serve hot or cold.

Chestnut Soufflé

(Serves 4)

(From Miss Briony Lill, Skegness, Lincs.)

---

1 lb. chestnuts
¼ pint milk
3 oz. sugar
3 eggs

1 oz. butter
almond essence
cream for serving (optional)

---

1. Peel chestnuts, stew in milk until tender, and liquidize or rub through a sieve. **2.** Warm purée in a saucepan and add sugar, butter, and flavouring. Take pan off heat and stir in egg yolks. **3.** Beat egg whites until stiff and gently fold in. **4.** Pour mixture into deep, buttered, 2-pint fire-proof dish and bake in moderate oven mark 5 (375° F.) for 40 minutes.

Date Meringue Tart (Serves 4)

(From Mrs. R. McMullan, Hertford, Herts.)

8 oz. shortcrust pastry
4 oz. large stoned dates
1 tablespoon brandy
  (optional)

3 egg whites
4 oz. caster sugar
2 oz. ground almonds

1. Line 8-inch flan tin with pastry. 2. Cut each date into four. Sprinkle with brandy and leave 20 minutes. 3. Beat egg whites until stiff; add almonds, caster sugar and drained dates to mixture. 4. Fill flan tin with mixture and bake in hot oven mark 6 (400° F.) for 25–30 minutes.

Eve's Pudding

1 lb. fruit in season	sponge mixture
3–4 oz. sugar	4 oz. self-raising flour
2 oz. soft margarine	1 egg
2 oz. sugar	1–2 tablespoons warm water

1. Stew fruit in very small quantity of water, sweetening to taste. **2.** Put the margarine, sugar, flour, and egg with 1 tablespoon warm water into mixing bowl and beat together for 2–3 minutes; if too stiff add further tablespoon warm water. **3.** Put fruit into base of oven-proof dish and cover with sponge mixture. **4.** Bake at mark 4 (350° F.) for about 40 minutes.

Apple Blossom Layer Pie

(Serves 8)

(From Miss S. Stansbie, Smethwick, Warley, Worcs.)

7-inch sweet pastry case
  (cooked)
First layer:
2 or 3 cooking apples
½ cup water
2 oz. sugar
12 stoned dates
Second layer:
½ can sweetened condensed
  milk
1 egg yolk
juice 1 lemon

Third layer:
1 dessertspoon gelatine
½ teaspoon lemon essence
1 egg white
juice from cooked apples
  made up to ¾ cupful with
  water
cochineal
double cream (whipped and
  sweetened)

1. Peel, core, and slice apples. **2.** Cook with sugar and water until soft, drain off syrup, and keep for third layer. Add dates to apple pulp, cool and put in pastry case. **3.** Beat condensed milk, egg yolk, and lemon juice together until well mixed and spread over apple layer. **4.** Soak gelatine well in cold apple syrup, dissolve over hot water, add lemon essence and few drops cochineal. Allow to cool and become partly set. **5.** Beat until light and fluffy, then fold in stiffly beaten egg white. Pile on top of pie and decorate with whipped cream sweetened with a little caster sugar.

Green Tomato Pie (Serves 4)

(From Mrs. T. Rayson, Oughterside, Carlisle)

8 oz. shortcrust pastry	2 oz. sugar
8 oz. green tomatoes	lemon juice

1. Roll out half of pastry and use to line a pie plate. **2.** Slice tomatoes finely and spread on pastry. Cover with sugar, moisten with lemon juice, cover with rest of pastry, and seal edges by rolling edge of pie with rolling pin. Prick top of pastry with fork. **3.** Bake for 15–20 minutes at mark 8 (450° F.). Serve hot or cold, with or without cream.

Banana Pudding

(Serves 6)

(From Mrs. B. M. Catterall, Worsley Hall, Wigan, Lancs.)

6 oz. flaky pastry
8 bananas
2 tablespoons apricot jam
2 oz. butter
3 oz. sugar

2 oz. cake crumbs
1 oz. desiccated coconut
1 large egg (separated)
juice and grated peel of 1
  lemon

1. Roll pastry out into strip and use to line sides of pie dish. Decorate edges and bake in hot oven mark 7 (425° F.). **2.** Mash bananas, mix with jam, and put into pastry case. **3.** Cream butter and sugar until soft and mix with egg yolk, lemon juice and grated rind, coconut and cake crumbs. Stiffly beat egg white and add to mixture, spread over fruit. **4.** Bake pudding for further 20 minutes at mark 6 (400° F.).

Hot Fruit Trifle (Serves 6)

(From Mrs. T. V. Magness, Harlech, Merionethshire)

12 oz. stewed fruit
4 small sponge cakes
1 pint thick custard
glacé cherries

For meringue:
3 oz. caster sugar
2 egg whites

1. Cut sponge cakes in half and line bottom of oven-proof dish with them. **2.** Cover with stewed fruit and pour thick custard on top. **3.** Whisk egg whites, fold in sugar with metal spoon, and whisk again until stiff. **4.** Pile meringue on top of mixture and seal the edges. **5.** Bake in slow oven mark $\frac{1}{2}$ (250° F.) for 20 minutes. When meringue is golden brown and set, remove from oven and decorate with chopped glacé cherries.

Apple Delight

(Serves 6)

(From Mrs. A. J. Deadman, Minster, Sheerness, Kent, who says it tastes just as good hot or cold)

2 lb. cooking apples
8 oz. self-raising flour
7 oz. porridge oats
5 oz. brown sugar
5 oz. granulated sugar

8 oz. stoned and chopped
  raisins
2 oz. finely chopped
  crystallized ginger
5 oz. margarine
pinch of salt

1. Grease and flour a 10×10-inch roasting tin. **2.** Sift flour and salt and rub in margarine; add oats and brown sugar. Sprinkle half of this dry mixture on bottom of roasting tin. **3.** Peel, core, and finely chop half of apples and put in baking tin. Sprinkle on half of granulated sugar, put raisins and ginger on top and repeat. **4.** Put remainder of oat mixture on top and press down. **5.** Bake in moderate oven mark 4 (375° F.) for 50–60 minutes. Serve with custard.

Lemon Meringue Pie

7-inch shortcrust pastry flan case (baked)	3 oz. caster sugar
2 lemons (grated peel and juice)	3 oz. granulated sugar
½ pint water	2 eggs (separated)
	1¼ oz. cornflour
	½ oz. margarine

1. Place lemon peel, juice, and most of water with granulated sugar in pan and bring to boil. **2.** Blend cornflour with remaining water and stir into hot liquid together with margarine. Cook for 2–3 minutes. **3.** Remove from heat and beat in egg yolks; spoon filling into pastry case. **4.** Whisk egg whites until stiff; then whisk in caster sugar; top pie with meringue. **5.** Bake at mark 3 (325° F.) until crisp and golden brown.

Macaron aux Pêches (Serves 6)

(From Joan Styles, Hounslow, Middlesex)

4 oz. grated almonds
8 oz. caster sugar
2 egg whites
½ oz. rice flour
½ teaspoon vanilla sugar
4 meringues
15 oz. tin peaches
rice paper

Chocolate sauce:
4 oz. plain chocolate
2 oz. butter
2 tablespoons sugar
½ gill hot water
pinch of salt
Decoration:
flaked almonds
4 tablespoons double cream
 (whipped)

1. Put almonds, caster sugar, egg whites, rice flour, and vanilla sugar into bowl and beat together well with a wooden spoon for 7–8 minutes. **2.** Put a sheet of rice paper onto a baking tray. Put mixture into a piping bag fitted with a large rose tube, pipe a round shape 8-inch diameter with a 1-inch deep border on the rice paper. **3.** Bake in oven at mark 5 (375° F.) for 20–30 minutes. Cool on wire rack and remove excess rice paper. **4.** Put chocolate, butter, water, sugar, and salt in pan and melt slowly, stirring all the time. When melted, boil until sauce thickens. **5.** Drain and chop peaches into squares. Add sauce and pour fruit and chocolate mixture into macaroon case. **6.** Crunch up meringues with cream and make a border around the edges on the chocolate. Decorate with flaked almonds.

Peach and Plenty Pudding

(Serves 4–6)

(From Mrs. H. Fagg, Leytonstone, London)

1 lb. peaches (fresh or
canned), halved and stoned
2–3 oz. sugar
2 tablespoons water
1 oz. hazelnuts (if bought
fresh, roast and remove
husks)

Sponge:
4 oz. self-raising flour
1 teaspoon baking powder
4 oz. soft margarine
2 eggs

Topping:
2 oz. plain flour
1 level teaspoon mixed spice
1 oz. margarine
2 oz. brown sugar
1 oz. roasted hazelnuts
2 tablespoons peach or
apricot jam

1. Place peaches, sugar, water, and hazelnuts in greased
2½-pint oven-proof dish. **2.** Sift flour and baking powder
together, add remaining sponge ingredients and beat for 2½
minutes. **3.** Spoon mixture over peaches and spread evenly.
4. Bake at mark 5 (375° F.) for 30–35 minutes, until sponge has
risen and turned golden. **5.** Sift flour and mixed spice together,
rub in margarine, and mix in sugar and nuts. **6.** When ready,
remove pudding from oven, quickly spread top with jam, then
sprinkle topping evenly over. **7.** Return pudding to oven for
further 10–15 minutes until topping is lightly browned. Serve
hot with cream, custard, or ice cream.

Pineapple Crumble

1 large tin crushed pineapple	3 oz. butter
6 oz. plain flour (sifted)	2 oz. caster sugar

1. Place pineapple in base of 2-pint oven-proof dish. **2.** Rub butter into flour, until texture is like fine breadcrumbs. Mix in sugar. **3.** Spoon crumble thickly over fruit and press down lightly with back of spoon. **4.** Bake at mark 5 (375° F.) for 15 minutes, then reduce to mark 4 (350° F.) for further 40 minutes, or until top is golden brown.

Pompadour Ring

(Serves 6)

(From Mrs. S. M. Farnham, St. Peter Port, Guernsey)

5 oz. self-raising flour
4½ oz. caster sugar
1 teaspoon baking powder
¼ teaspoon salt
7 tablespoons corn oil
2 eggs
2 tablespoons milk
vanilla essence to taste
lard to grease mould

Filling:
2 large cans fruit or fresh fruit
¼ pint syrup
3 tablespoons rum or sherry (optional)
spiked almonds
¼ pint cream (whipped)

1. Beat oil into eggs, milk and vanilla. **2.** Sift dry ingredients together. Pour liquid into mixture and beat well together for 3 minutes. **3.** Pour into greased ring mould and bake at mark 4 (350° F.) for 20–30 minutes. **4.** Stand sponge ring on cooling tray and prick all over with skewer. Mix syrup and rum together and pour over sponge, taking care not to make it too wet. **5.** Place ring on serving dish and fill centre with mixed fruit. Place almonds all around the ring, decorate with whipped cream and serve remaining syrup separately.

Harvest Pudding

(From Mrs. G. Rose, Frowlesworth, Rugby, who recommends it for times when apples are cheap—and as 'a winner with the menfolk')

slices of buttered bread, as needed
1 lb. cooking apples
2 oz. suet
3 oz. brown sugar
3 oz. seedless raisins

1 oz. chopped nuts
2 eggs
grated lemon rind
1 cup milk
caster sugar

1. Grease and line dish with bread and butter. **2.** Slice apples, mix with suet, raisins, nuts, sugar, and lemon rind. **3.** Fill pie dish with mixture and cover with more bread and butter. **4.** Beat eggs, add to milk, and pour over top. Cover and stand. (At least 1½ hours, or overnight.) **5.** Bake in moderate oven mark 4 (350° F.) for 1 hour. Sprinkle with caster sugar and serve.

Rhubarb and Gingerbread Ring

(Serves 4–6)

(From Mrs. I. M. Smith, Werrington, Peterborough)

9 oz. plain flour
1 level teaspoon mixed spice
2 level teaspoons ground
 ginger
3 oz. soft brown sugar
4 oz. lard
4 oz. black treacle
4 oz. golden syrup
1 standard egg

1 level teaspoon bicarbonate
 of soda
Filling:
1 lb. rhubarb
1 level tablespoon cornflour
4 level tablespoons caster
 sugar
¼ pint water

1. Prepare oven mark 4 (350° F.). Grease an 8-inch ring tin or jelly mould. (Or use an 8-inch cake tin with a weighted cocoa tin in the centre.) **2.** Sift flour and spices into bowl and add sugar. Warm milk in a small saucepan and pour into a jug. Place lard, treacle, and syrup in same saucepan and heat unil lard has melted. (Dust scale-pan with about 1 teaspoon flour mixture before weighing treacle and syrup.) **3.** Beat egg in small bowl, add bicarbonate of soda and warmed milk, stir until dissolved. Pour egg and treacle mixtures into centre of dry ingredients; beat until smooth. Pour into prepared tin and place on baking sheet. **4.** Bake just below centre of oven for 50 minutes to 1 hour. Test by pressing with fingers: if cooked, gingerbread should spring back and have begun to shrink from sides of tin. **5.** Wash and cut rhubarb into short lengths and place in a 2-pint pie dish. Blend cornflour and sugar with water and pour over rhubarb. Cover with foil and cook in oven with gingerbread for the final 30–40 minutes of cooking time. Remove gingerbread from oven and leave to cool for 10 minutes. **6.** Using a round-bladed knife, loosen edges of gingerbread and turn out on to a warm dish. Spoon rhubarb and sauce into centre of gingerbread ring. Serve warm with cream or custard.

Mincemeat Surprise (Serves 4)

(From Mrs. B. Latham, Stafford)

Pudding:
2 oz. margarine
2 oz. caster sugar
1 egg (unbeaten)
1 large teaspoon milk
finely grated rind of $\frac{1}{2}$ lemon
2 oz. self-raising flour
1 level teaspoon baking
  powder

Filling:
1 level tablespoon lemon curd
1 rounded tablespoon
  mincemeat
2 egg whites
4 oz. caster sugar

1. Beat all pudding ingredients together thoroughly for one minute, turn into greased 7-inch sandwich tin and bake in a moderate oven mark 4 (350° F.) for 20–25 minutes. **2.** Turn out and slice in half while still hot. Sandwich with lemon curd and spread mincemeat on top. **3.** Place on oven-proof dish and cover with stiffly beaten egg whites and sugar, saving a little sugar to sprinkle on top. **4.** Bake for a further 20 minutes in a warm oven mark 2 (300° F.).

Treacle Tart

(Serves 4)

6 oz. shortcrust pastry
2 level tablespoons fresh
white breadcrumbs
2 level tablespoons black
treacle

1 level tablespoon golden
syrup
1 level teaspoon grated lemon
peel
1 dessertspoon lemon juice

1. Use pastry to line 8-inch pie plate, trim and crimp edges.
2. Mix together crumbs, treacle, syrup, lemon peel, and juice;
spread over pastry to within 1 inch of edges. **3.** Roll out pastry
trimmings and cut into thin strips; moisten edges of tart and
arrange in strips in lattice design over filling, pressing edges
on to pastry rim firmly. **4.** Bake at mark 6 (400° F.) for 30 minutes
or until pastry is golden brown.

Try a Treat for Teatime

When you look at this section you'll see why the English cake can really be considered a work of art. There are more exotic recipes too, brought back from holiday or the writer's home country.

14-Carat Cake

(From Mrs. L. Byrne, Chadwell Heath, Romford, Essex)

8 oz. plain flour
2 teaspoons baking powder
1½ teaspoons bicarbonate of
 soda
1 teaspoon salt
2 teaspoons cinnamon
8 oz. caster sugar
1¼ cups vegetable oil
4 eggs

2 cups finely grated carrots
8½ oz. can pineapple (drained
 and crushed)
2 oz. chopped walnuts
Frosting:
2 oz. softened butter
8 oz. soft cream cheese
1 teaspoon vanilla essence
1 lb. sifted icing sugar

1. Sift together flour, soda, baking powder, salt, and cinnamon. **2.** Add sugar, oil, eggs, and mix well. Add carrots, nuts, pineapple and mix again. **3.** Bake in three 9-inch layer pans (greased and floured) at mark 4 (350° F.) for about 40 minutes. Cool a little, then turn out of pans to cool completely. **4.** Cream together butter, cream cheese, and vanilla, then beat in icing sugar until smooth. **5.** Spread frosting mixture between each layer, sandwich together, and spread on top also. Dust with cinnamon.

Black Beer Cake

(From Mrs. L. J. Bottomley, Middlestown, Wakefield, Yorks.)

6 oz. self-raising flour
2 oz. ground almonds
12 oz. mixed dried fruit
4 oz. butter or margarine

4 oz. sugar
1 beaten egg
4 fl. oz. stout or Guinness

1. Simmer fruit, sugar, butter, and stout together in fairly large pan for 20 minutes and allow to cool. **2.** Add beaten egg, ground almonds, and self-raising flour. **3.** Turn into greased 7-inch tin and bake for 2½ hours at mark 1 (275° F.).

Bourbon Biscuits

4 oz. plain flour
½ level teaspoon baking
  powder
½ oz. cocoa
2 oz. butter
2 oz. caster sugar
1 level tablespoon golden
  syrup

Filling:
1 oz. plain chocolate (melted)
1½ tablespoons water
2 oz. icing sugar (sifted)
vanilla essence to taste

1. Sift together flour, baking powder, and cocoa. **2.** Cream butter and sugar until light and fluffy and beat in syrup. Stir in half flour mixture. **3.** Turn dough on to working surface and knead in remaining flour mixture. **4.** Roll out to ¼ inch thick on greaseproof paper, sprinkle top with granulated sugar and press in with rolling pin. Cut dough into neat fingers—1 × 2½ inches—and carefully lift on to greased baking sheet. **4.** Prick each biscuit two or three times and bake at mark 3 (325° F.) for 15–20 minutes. Cool. **5.** Beat all ingredients for filling together, making sure mixture is cool and a soft consistency before sandwiching biscuits in pairs.

Brandy Snaps

2 oz. plain flour (sifted)
1 level teaspoon ground
  ginger (sifted)
finely grated rind ½ lemon
2 oz. butter

2 oz. soft brown sugar
3 level tablespoons golden
  syrup
1 teaspoon lemon juice
whipped cream for filling

1. Mix together flour, ginger, and lemon rind. **2.** Melt butter, sugar, and syrup together in pan, then stir in flour mixture and lemon juice. **3.** Line baking tray with silicone paper and drop up to six ½ teaspoons of the mixture, well apart, on to paper, allowing plenty of room for spreading. **4.** Bake at mark 5 (375° F.) for 10 minutes. **5.** Remove brandy snaps from paper and roll each loosely round handle of greased wooden spoon. Repeat baking process until mixture is all used. Allow to cool. **6.** Pipe rosette of whipped cream inside each end and serve. Can be stored, without cream, in an airtight tin.

Cereal Fruit Loaf

(From Mrs. E. M. England, Rease Heath, Nantwich, Cheshire)

2 oz. crumbled Weetabix or
  Co-op whole wheat cereal
8 oz. soft brown sugar
6 oz. mixed dried fruit
1 oz. finely chopped walnuts

½ pint milk
1 egg
7 oz. self-raising flour
¼ teaspoon salt

1. Soak Weetabix, sugar, and dried fruit in milk for 6–12 hours.
2. Add the egg, self-raising flour, and walnuts and mix together.
3. Turn into greased loaf tin and bake for 1–1½ hours at mark 3 (325° F.). Slice and serve plain or buttered.

Chocolate Eclairs

2½ oz. plain flour
¼ pint water
4 oz. butter
pinch salt

2 standard eggs (well beaten)
whipped cream for filling
¼ lb. dark chocolate (melted)

1. Sift together flour and salt. **2.** Slowly melt 2 oz. butter with water in pan over low heat and bring to brisk boil. Lower heat and add flour to pan, beating well until mixture leaves sides of pan to form soft ball consistency. Cool slightly. **3.** Gradually blend in eggs, beating hard until shiny—this improves texture of pastry. **4.** Place pastry in forcing bag fitted with ½-inch plain nozzle and pipe 12×4-inch lengths on to greased baking tray. **5.** Bake at mark 6 (400° F.) for 10 minutes, then reduce to mark 4 (350° F.) for further 20 minutes. Remove from oven and allow to cool. **6.** Beat remaining 2 oz. butter into hot melted chocolate. Slit eclairs and fill with cream. Spread the chocolate on top and allow to set before serving.

Date with a Banana Cake

(From Miss M. Pike, Westcliff-on-Sea, Essex)

---

7 oz. self-raising flour
$\frac{1}{4}$ teaspoon bicarbonate of soda
$\frac{1}{2}$ teaspoon salt
2 teaspoons mixed spice

8 oz. peeled bananas
4 oz. dates
2 eggs
$3\frac{1}{2}$ oz. margarine
6 oz. caster sugar

---

1. Pre-heat oven to mark 4 (350° F.). **2.** Grease and flour an 8-inch cake tin, preferably with removable base. **3.** Sieve flour, bicarbonate of soda, salt, and spice twice to make sure they are well mixed. **4.** Mash bananas and roughly chop dates. **5.** Using a large bowl, cream sugar and margarine and add one egg. Beat thoroughly, add other egg and beat again. **6.** Mix in mashed bananas and chopped dates; finally fold in flour and put into prepared tin. Bake in centre of oven for approximately $1\frac{1}{4}$ hours. (May be iced if liked.)

Christmas or Birthday Cake

(From Mrs. G. E. Trent, Dorchester, Dorset, a rich and expensive cake for high days and holidays)

8 oz. butter
6 oz. caster sugar
2 tablespoons golden syrup
4 or 5 eggs
a few drops almond essence
10 oz. plain flour
½ teaspoon baking powder
pinch salt
2 oz. ginger

2 oz. ground almonds
2 oz. walnuts
Glacé and crystallized fruit:
4 oz. pineapple
4 oz. apricots
4 oz. pears
4 oz. peaches
2 oz. cherries
2 oz. angelica

1. Grease and line an 8-inch cake tin. **2.** Cut all glacé and crystallized fruit, chop walnuts, and mix with a small amount of flour. **3.** Cream butter and sugar, beat in eggs one at a time, add syrup and almond essence. **4.** Sift flour, baking powder, and salt, and fold into mixture. **5.** Finally fold in the prepared fruit and nuts. **6.** Place in tin, hollow out centre, and bake in oven at mark 3 (350° F.) for 2½ hours. If browning too quickly after 1½ hours cover top with double greaseproof paper. Cover with almond paste and royal icing if desired. Can be eaten after two days, or will keep for three or four months.

Christmas Bunloaves

(From Mrs. Margaret Edwards, Everton, Liverpool, who says the recipe has been handed down in her family for over eighty years)

2 lb. plain flour
1 lb. soft brown sugar
½ lb. white sugar
2 teaspoons baking powder
4 teaspoons mixed spice
2 teaspoons ground nutmeg
1 teaspoon ground ginger
½ lb. lard
½ lb. margarine

½ lb. raisins (stoned and chopped)
½ lb. sultanas
1 lb. currants
2 oz. chopped glacé cherries
2 oz. candied peel
½ pint milk (or slightly more)
5 eggs
½ teaspoon almond essence
lemon juice

1. Mix dry ingredients together, rub in fat, add fruit and candied peel. **2.** Beat up eggs in milk, add essence and few drops lemon juice. **3.** Mix all together until moist but not too stiff. **4.** Line two large loaf tins, pour mixture in and cover well with greaseproof paper. To give a shiny top, pat a little milk gently over top before covering. Bake at mark 3 (325° F.) for 3 hours. Will make two 3½-lb. loaves.

Flapjack Biscuits

¼ lb. butter
3 oz. golden syrup
3 oz. soft brown sugar

6 oz. porridge oats
1 oz. desiccated coconut
1 oz. chopped walnuts

1. Place butter, syrup, and sugar in pan over low heat until melted; stir in oats, coconut, and nuts. **2.** Spread thinly over base of greased 9×12-inch Swiss roll tin and smooth top. **3.** Bake at mark 4 (350° F.) for 30 minutes and leave to cool 5 minutes in tin. Cut into 24 fingers and remove from tin when cold.

Eccles Cakes

½ oz. butter
2 oz. currants
1 oz. chopped mixed peel
1 oz. soft brown sugar

½ level teaspoon mixed spice
7 oz. flaky or puff pastry
milk to glaze
caster sugar

1. Melt butter in saucepan, stir in currants, peel, brown sugar, and spice. **2.** Roll out pastry thinly and cut into rounds using a plain pastry cutter. **3.** Put heaped teaspoon of filling on each circle, moisten edges with water, and draw up to enclose filling. Seal well. **4.** Turn over, roll out to about ½-inch thickness, prick over top with fork and brush with milk. Sprinkle caster sugar over. **5.** Bake at mark 7 (425° F.) for 15–20 minutes.

Honey and Oat Cake

(From Mrs. J. D. Woollam, Acocks Green, Birmingham)

4 oz. margarine
3 oz. caster sugar
4 oz. pure honey

2 large eggs
4 oz. porridge oats
4 oz. self-raising flour

1. Line a 7-inch cake tin and preheat oven to mark 4 (350° F.).
2. Cream margarine, add sugar and cream well. **3.** Add eggs and beat until well mixed and full of small bubbles, then add honey and mix gently. **4.** Add alternating small amounts of oats and flour and fold in gently. If the mixture is too stiff add a little milk. **5.** Pour into cake tin, smooth surface and place in centre of oven and bake for 45 minutes. A knife can be inserted and withdrawn clean when the cake is cooked. Allow to cool and serve sliced and spread with butter.

French Hazelnut Slice

(From Mrs. S. Ballester, Bournemouth, Hants., who says the original French recipe was for walnuts but she thinks the hazelnut flavour is nicer)

2 large eggs
4 oz. sugar
2½ oz. self-raising flour
¼ pint single cream

2½ oz. ground hazelnuts
1 teaspoon baking powder
melted dark chocolate to
 glaze
whole hazelnuts

1. Mix eggs, sugar, and cream well, add sifted flour and baking powder and lastly hazelnuts. **2.** Bake in buttered and lined 9-inch square tin for about 30–35 minutes at mark 5 (375° F.). **3.** When cool turn out cake and cut in two (making oblong halves), glaze with melted chocolate, and decorate with a few whole hazelnuts.

Gâteau à la Trouville

From Mrs. Doreen King, Boston, Lincs.)

2 eggs
3 oz. caster sugar
2 oz. sifted plain flour
pinch baking powder
½ pint double cream
vanilla essence

For caramel sauce:
2 oz. granulated sugar
½ pint single cream
3 tablespoons water

1. Separate yolk and whites of eggs, beat yolks and sugar until thick. Whip whites until stiff and mix with other batter alternately with a spoonful of flour. Then carefully add baking powder. **2.** Bake in moderate oven mark 5 (375° F.) in sandwich tin for approximately 20 minutes or until well risen and firm to the touch. **3.** When cool scoop out centre and fill with stiffly beaten cream flavoured with vanilla. **4.** To make sauce, dissolve sugar in saucepan until golden brown. Very carefully, ensuring hands are covered, add water. Cool slightly, pour onto cream and stir until quite smooth. Chill and pour over gâteau.

Gugelhuff

(From Mrs. E. Wertheim, London N.W.2, a cake recipe which is a firm favourite in Germany and Austria and for which a cylindrical cake mould is needed)

---

8 oz. self-raising flour
1 tablespoon cornflour
3 eggs (separated)
5 tablespoons milk
4oz. sugar
4 oz. butter or margarine

3 oz. sultanas
1 oz. grated almonds
1 large teaspoon rum
grated rind and juice of 1
  orange

---

1. Soak sultanas, if possible the evening before, in orange juice and rind. **2.** Warm butter. **3.** Put a little flour, mixed with cornflour, sugar, egg yolks, and milk into butter. Beat very well. Repeat until everything is used up, stir in sultanas, juice, and rind. **4.** Beat egg whites until very stiff and fold into mixture. **5.** Thoroughly grease a cylindrical cake mould (use butter, not margarine), sprinkle with grated almonds and turn mixture into it. **6.** Bake at mark 5 (375° F.) for about 1 hour. Allow cake 10 minutes to cool in oven, then remove to wire tray. Dust with icing sugar.

Apple Lemon Surprises

(From Mrs. J. Day, Felixstowe, Suffolk)

---

1 lb. cooking apples
½ lb. caster sugar
1 oz. butter

a little ground nutmeg
juice and grated rind of a
  lemon

---

1. Peel, core, and stew apples. **2.** Rub through sieve and add sugar, butter, nutmeg, and grated rind and juice of lemon. Stir all together over heat for a few minutes. **3.** Whip up thoroughly until the mixture is stiff and drop in dessertspoons onto a greased oven tray. **4.** Bake in a cool oven mark ½ (250° F.) until set, about 15–20 minutes. Can be kept like biscuits in airtight tin.

Wacky Cake

(From Mrs. Nora Rawlinson, Tyldesley, Lancs., who brought the recipe back from Malaya and says it 'defies all baking rules!')

4 oz. sugar
3 oz. plain flour
¼ teaspoon salt
½ oz. cocoa
1 teaspoon bicarbonate of
  soda

1 teaspoon vanilla essence
⅓ cup cooking oil
¼ pint cold water
1 tablespoon vinegar

1. Sift together all dry ingredients. **2.** Add oil, water, vinegar and vanilla essence and stir mixture until smooth. **3.** Turn into ungreased square or oblong tin (size approximately 9×13×2 inches) and bake for 30–35 minutes at mark 4 (350° F.). Can be eaten hot or cold.

Mount Pleasant Cake

(From Mrs. M. Barnes, Barnoldswick, Lancs.)

---

6 oz. caster sugar	1 oz. corn flour
4 oz. butter or margarine	1 oz. ground almonds
2 oz. self-raising flour	2 eggs
2 oz. ground rice	

---

1. Cream butter and sugar, add eggs, then mix in remaining ingredients. **2.** Turn into square tin about 7 × 7 × 3 inches and lightly sprinkle top with caster sugar. **3.** Bake at mark 4 (350° F.) until firm to touch. When cold cut into squares.

Nut Eclairs

(From Mrs. M. Wilson, Cowdenbeath, Fife, Scotland)

2 oz. plain chocolate
5 oz. porridge oats
3 tablespoons sugar
1½ oz. margarine

2 tablespoons golden syrup
1 teaspoon vanilla essence
½ level teaspoon salt
2 oz. chopped nuts

1. Melt chocolate and margarine in basin over pan of hot water. Add all other ingredients except nuts and mix thoroughly. **2.** Turn mixture into shallow 7×7-inch greased tin and sprinkle nuts on top. **3.** Bake in hot oven mark 7 (425° F.) for 10–15 minutes. When ready, make into fingers and leave to cool. Divide into portions.

Orange Cake

½ lb. butter
½ lb. caster sugar
4 large eggs
½ lb. plain flour

grated rind of 1 orange
½ lb. icing sugar
orange juice (about 3
   dessertspoons)

1. Grease and line 7-inch cake tin. **2.** Cream butter and sugar together until light and fluffy. **3.** Beat in eggs one at a time, adding 1 tablespoon flour with each; gently fold in remaining flour and orange peel. **3.** Transfer to prepared tin and bake at mark 3 (325° F.) for 1¾–2 hours. Leave in tin 5 minutes before turning out. **4.** Make orange icing by mixing together icing sugar and sufficient orange juice to give coating consistency. Spread over top of cake when cool.

Oat Cookies

(From Mrs. D. Smith, Lower Broadheath, Worcester)

1 egg
4 oz. porridge oats
2 oz. ground almonds

3 oz. butter or margarine
3 oz. raisins
3 oz. golden syrup

1. Melt butter and golden syrup, pour into dry ingredients and stir. Add raisins and egg and mix well. **2.** Pour into shallow greased 7-inch square tin and bake at mark 4 (350° F.) for 15–20 minutes. Leave in tin and cut into pieces in tin also. Turn on to wire rack when cold.

Pumpkin Scones

(From Mrs. Watkins, Old Town, Croydon)

---

10 oz. plain flour
2 level teaspoons baking
  powder
½ cup mashed pumpkin **or**
  melon

1 egg
2 oz. butter
2 oz. suggar
¼ pint milk

---

1. Cream butter and sugar together, add pumpkin or melon and the egg, well beaten. **2.** Slowly add milk. **3.** Add flour, sifted with baking powder, and mix well. **4.** Knead lightly on floured board and roll out to 1½ inches thick. **5.** Cut into small rounds, place on floured tray and cook for 20 minutes at mark 6 (400° F.). Place on rack to cool.

Rich Chocolate Cake

(From Mrs. B. Johns, Tewkesbury, Gloucestershire)

½ lb. plain chocolate (melted)
5 eggs (separated)
1½ oz. self-raising flour
3 oz. ground almonds
6½ oz. granulated sugar
4 oz. butter or margarine

Filling: apricot jam
Icing: ½ lb. plain chocolate
(optional)

1. Melt chocolate. **2.** Separate eggs, beat up whites until stiff, and lightly beat yolks. **3.** Cream butter and sugar until light and fluffy. Add egg yolks and melted chocolate, ground almonds, and flour. Loosely fold in egg whites. **4.** Put in well-greased 8-inch cake tin and bake for 1¼ hours in moderate oven mark 4 (350° F.). The cake should be moist and gooey—don't overbake. **5.** When cold cut through middle and sandwich together with thin layer of apricot jam. Ice with melted chocolate if desired.

Siena Cake

(From Miss P. Manning, Southend-on-Sea, Essex, who discovered it on holiday in the old Italian town of Siena—and persuaded a hotel waiter to give her the recipe)

$3\frac{1}{2}$ oz. self-raising flour
1 level tablespoon
  unsweetened cocoa
1 level teaspoon cinnamon
1 level teaspoon nutmeg
4 oz. chopped, candied peel
1 lemon
rice paper

2 oz. almonds ⎫
1 oz. walnuts ⎬ shelled
3 oz. hazelnuts ⎭ weight
3 tablespoons honey
3 oz. sugar
Topping:
3 tablespoons icing sugar
1 teaspoon cinnamon

---

1. Lightly grease shallow 7-inch round cake tin and line base with rice paper. **2.** Roughly chop nuts, keeping pieces fairly large, and mix chopped candied peel and rind grated from lemon. **3.** Sieve flour with spices and cocoa and stir nuts and peel into it. **4.** Squeeze juice from lemon into a saucepan with honey. Add sugar and heat slowly until sugar dissolves. Stirring continuously, boil gently for a few minutes until syrup becomes quite tacky (soft ball stage). Pour over other ingredients and stir—it should form a sticky, rather solid mass. **5.** Spoon into prepared tin and bake at mark 3 (325° F.) for about 35–40 minutes. When cool, sprinkle with icing sugar mixed with cinnamon, and preferably store in airtight tin for two or three days before eating.

Swedish Oat Wafers

(Will make up to 30)

(From Mrs. Inga Forgan, Guildford, Surrey, a recipe from Sweden which makes a good accompaniment to ice cream or mousse)

2½ oz. porridge oats	1 egg
2½ oz. butter	1 teaspoon plain flour
4 oz. caster sugar	1 teaspoon baking powder

---

1. Melt butter and pour while still hot over oats. Add rest of ingredients after oats and butter have cooled a little; flour and baking powder should only be added just before baking.
2. Have several baking sheets ready and grease well with cold butter or margarine. Put small dollops of mixture, well spaced out, on baking sheet (no more than four on an average-sized baking sheet). Bake in low oven mark 3 (325° F.) until light brown (8–10 minutes). While baking, mixture will spread in a way similar to brandy snaps for example. Have ready an oiled rolling pin or milk bottle. Cut wafers quickly from baking sheets using a broad, thin knife or slice, then place over rolling pin to shape. Should they harden too quickly to get off sheet, put back into oven for a minute or two. These wafers keep very well in an airtight tin.

Sweet and Sour Cookies

(From Mrs. H. Karkling, Low Hill, Wolverhampton)

---

8 oz. plain flour
4 oz. soft margarine
4 oz. sugar
1 carton flavoured,
  sweetened yoghurt (to
  taste)

porridge oats or crushed
  breakfast cereal (any kind)
glacé cherries or walnuts
  to decorate

---

1. Mix margarine, sugar, and flour well together and stir in yoghurt. **2.** Add enough cereal or oats to give a 'rock-cake' consistency. (Chopped dried fruits or glacé cherries may also be used if liked.) **3.** Put mixture in little heaps on greased baking trays and decorate tops with cherries or walnuts. Bake in top of oven mark 6 (400° F.) until lightly browned and firm to touch, approximately 20 minutes. (When cool they can be topped with melted chocolate or glacé icing; in this case decoration should be added afterwards.)

Viennese Biscuits

4 oz. butter or block margarine
1 oz. icing sugar
4 oz. plain flour

vanilla essence
glacé cherries

1. Cream butter and sugar together until light and fluffy; stir in few drops vanilla essence and gradually work in sifted flour. **2.** Put mixture into piping bag fitted with rose piping-tube and pipe fingers or rounds on to greased tray. Decorate each biscuit with piece of glacé cherry. **3.** Bake at mark 4 (350° F.) for 15–20 minutes or until lightly browned. Leave on tray for few minutes before removing to cooling tray.

Walnut Fudge Cake

(From Mrs. B. Line, Felixstowe, Suffolk, who says it is 'an invention which has proved a favourite')

Cake:
2 oz. margarine
5 oz. caster sugar
few drops vanilla essence
2 large eggs
2 oz. chopped walnuts
3 tablespoons milk
5 oz. plain flour
1½ level teaspoons baking powder
pinch salt

Decoration and filling:
6 oz. butter
2 tablespoons milk
1 level tablespoon malted
  milk powder
12 oz. sifted icing sugar
2 oz. coffee sugar crystals

1. Grease two 7½-inch sandwich tins and line with greased greaseproof paper. **2.** Beat margarine in mixing bowl until smooth, add caster sugar and cream together until light and fluffy. **3.** Separate eggs, keeping whites, and beat yolks into creamed mixture with vanilla essence; stir in chopped walnuts and milk. Sift flour, baking powder, and salt together and fold into mixture with metal spoon. **4.** Whisk egg whites into stiff peaks and fold carefully into mixture. **5.** Divide mixture between tins and level surfaces. Bake on centre shelf of moderate oven mark 5 (375° F.) for 20–25 minutes, until springy to the touch and starting to shrink from sides of tin. Turn on to wire tray and leave to cool. **6.** Melt the butter in pan over low heat, add milk and malted milk powder. **7.** Remove pan from heat and gradually beat in icing sugar; when smooth leave to cool and thicken. **8.** Peel paper from bottom of sponge and sandwich together with half of icing. Spread remaining icing on top of cake, letting it flow slightly over sides and sprinkle with sugar crystals. Leave in cool place until needed.

Mmmm . . . Cake

(From Mrs. L. Sperrink, Edwinstowe, Mansfield, Notts., who devised it herself and says 'it has all the flavour of Christmas or Party Cake, without being expensive')

8 oz. self-raising flour
4 oz. soft margarine
4 oz. sugar
1 egg

8 oz. mincemeat
1½ dessertspoons marmalade
2 oz. sliced glacé cherries
2 teaspoons sherry (optional)

1. Cream margarine and sugar until light and fluffy. **2.** Add marmalade and beat again. **3.** Beat egg and add to creamed mixture. **4.** Fold in flour. **5.** Add mincemeat, sliced cherries and sherry. **6.** Turn into well-greased 6-inch cake tin and bake in oven at mark 3 (325° F.) for approximately 1½ hours, until firm to the touch. Turn upside down on tray to cool. Will keep several weeks in airtight tin.

CONTRIBUTOR	RECIPE
Miss E. Atkin Sketty, Swansea	Pensioner's Casserole
Mrs. M. Aunger Colne, Lancashire	Giblet Pie
Miss J. Austen Walney Island, Barrow-in-Furness, Lancashire	Bacon Extravaganza
Miss B. Bailey Lancing, Sussex	Sage and Onion Pudding
Mrs. S. Ballester Bournemouth, Hampshire	French Hazelnut Slice
Mrs. M. Barnes Barnoldswick, Lancashire	Mount Pleasant Cake
Mrs. D. Bell Eastleigh, Hampshire	Golden Bake
Mrs. L. J. Bottomley Middlestown, Wakefield, Yorkshire	Black Beer Cake
Mrs. L. Byrne Chadwell Heath, Romford, Essex	14-Carat Cake
Mrs. B. M. Catterall Worsley Hall, Wigan, Lancashire	Banana Pudding
Mrs. C. Coleman Buckden, Huntingdonshire	Roasted Fruity Lamb
Mrs. S. Courteney Westcliff-on-Sea, Essex	Baked Dumpling Surprise
Mrs. J. Day Felixstowe, Suffolk	Apple Lemon Surprises
Mrs. A. J. Deadman Minster, Sheerness, Kent	Apple Delight
Mrs. M. Edwards Everton, Liverpool	Christmas Bun-loaves
Mrs. E. M. England Rease Heath, Nantwich, Cheshire	Cereal Fruit Loaf
Mrs. R. Evans Llandrillo, Corwen, Merioneth	Southern Fish Bake
Mrs. H. Fagg Leytonstone, London	Peach and Plenty Pudding
Mrs. S. M. Farnham St. Peter Port, Guernsey	Pompadour Ring
Mrs. Flisher Maidstone, Kent	Honey Tart
Mrs. I. Forgan Guildford, Surrey	Swedish Oat Wafers
Mrs. K. Halton St. Helens, Lancashire	Cheese Meringue Pie

CONTRIBUTOR	RECIPE
Mrs. A. Hills Bourne, Lincolnshire	Cowboy Lunch
Mrs. B. Hirst Wath-on-Dearne, Yorkshire	Shrimp Flan
Mrs. I. Hitchon St. Peters, Broadstairs, Kent	Mock Roast
Mrs. E. Hollingworth Whitestone, Exeter, Devonshire	Short, Short Pastry
Mrs. J. S. Hopper Frodsham, Cheshire	Cheese Whispers
Mrs. E. Hurlock Plumstead, London	Salmon Pie
Mrs. B. Johns Tewkesbury, Gloucestershire	Rich Chocolate Cake
Mrs. H. Karkling Low Hill, Wolverhampton	Sweet and Sour Cookies
Mrs. D. King Boston, Lincolnshire	Gâteau à la Trouville
Mrs. B. Knowles Richmond, Yorkshire	Monday Bake
Mrs. B. Latham Stafford	Mincemeat Surprise
Miss B. Lill Skegness, Lincolnshire	Chestnut Soufflé
Mrs. B. Line Felixstowe, Suffolk	Walnut Fudge Cake
Miss R. Lock Cirencester, Gloucestershire	Gypsy Pie
Miss R. M. Lord Redbridge, Ilford, Essex	Tripe Casserole
Mrs. R. McMullan Hertford, Hertfordshire	Date Meringue Tart
Mrs. T. V. Magness Harlech, Merionethshire	Hot Fruit Trifle
Miss P. Manning Southend-on-Sea, Essex	Siena Cake
Mrs. G. D. Nicholas Chelmsley Wood, Birmingham	Plum Wheels
Mrs. M. Oliver Flint, Wales	Horseshoe Surprise
Mrs. G. Osborn Ashby, Scunthorpe, Lincolnshire	Apple Almond Pie
Mr. E. J. Page St. Albans, Hertfordshire	Mushroom and Celery Pie
Mrs. R. Parkinson Doncaster, Yorkshire	Bacon and Egg Pie

CONTRIBUTOR	RECIPE
Miss M. Pike Westcliff-on-Sea, Essex	Date with a Banana Cake
Mrs. M. Radford Stretford, Lancashire	Tattee 'Oggie
Mrs. D. Ransome Kings Lynn, Norfolk	Banana and Raisin Pie
Mrs. T. Rayson Oughterside, Carlisle	Green Tomato Pie
Mrs. G. Rose Frowlesworth, Warwickshire	Harvest Pudding
Mrs. N. Rawlinson Tyldesley, Lancashire	Wacky Cake
Mrs. E. Shreeve Frinton-on-Sea, Essex	Quick Salmon Pie
Mrs. D. Smith Lower Broadheath, Worcestershire	Oat Cookies
Mrs. I. M. Smith Werrington, Peterborough	Rhubarb and Gingerbread Ring
Mrs. V. Smith Waddon, Croydon, Surrey	Chicken Cooked in Cider
Mrs. L. Sperrink Edwinstowe, Mansfield, Nottinghamshire	Mmmm ... Cake
Miss S. Stansbie Smethwick, Warley, Worcestershire	Apple Blossom Layer Pie
Mrs. J. Stroud Lee, London	Banana Doolittle
Mrs. J. Styles Hounslow, Middlesex	Macaron aux Pêches
Mrs. E. Taylor North Cotes, Grimsby, Lincolnshire	Creole Rabbit Pie
Mrs. G. E. Trent Dorchester, Dorset	Christmas or Birthday Cake
Miss Y. Tulinski Leicester	Shepherd's Pie with Marrow
Mrs. Watkins Old Town, Croydon	Pumpkin Scones
Mrs. E. Websdale Bloxham, Banbury, Oxfordshire	Macaroni Slices
Mrs. E. Wertheim London N.W.2	Gugelhuff
Mrs. M. Wilson Cowdenbeath, Fife, Scotland	Nut Eclairs
Mrs. J. D. Woollam Acocks Green, Birmingham	Honey and Oat Cake

Metric Measures

A straight conversion of Imperial measures to metric gives unusable fractions. This chart shows metric equivalents to the nearest 5 grammes.

ounces	grammes
1	30
2	55
3	85
4	115
5	140
6	170
7	200
8	225
9	255
10	285
11	310
12	340
13	370
14	400
15	425
16	455

1 teaspoon	5 millilitres
1 dessertspoon	10 millilitres
1 tablespoon	15 millilitres

Metric Measures

pints	millilitres
$\frac{1}{4}$	142
$\frac{1}{3}$	189
$\frac{1}{2}$	284
1	568
2	1,136

inches	centimetres
(1 inch = 2·54 cm)	
$\frac{1}{8}$	$\frac{1}{4}$
$\frac{1}{4}$	$\frac{1}{2}$
$\frac{1}{2}$	1
1	$2\frac{1}{2}$
2	5
3	$7\frac{1}{2}$
4	10
5	13
6	15
7	18
8	20
9	23
10	26
11	28
12	30

Oven
Temperatures

food type	°C	°F	gas no	oven heat
meringues keeping food hot	110°C	225°F	$\frac{1}{4}$	very cool
fruit bottling	130°C	250°F	$\frac{1}{2}$	very cool
custards, egg dishes, milk puddings	140°C	275°F	1	cool
stews, rich fruit cakes	150°C	300°F	2	slow
slow roasting, plain fruit cakes	170°C	325°F	3	moderately slow
Victoria sponge cakes, biscuits, madeira cake	180°C	350°F	4	moderate
whisked sponges, small cakes	190°C	375°F	5	moderately hot
shortcrust pastry, tarts	200°C	400°F	6	hot
quick roasting, scones, bread	220°C	425°F	7	very hot
flaky and puff pastry, buns, rolls	230°C	450°F	8	very hot

notes

"

Shopping's quite simple . . .
you buy what you want:
and the shop takes the profit.
It's the same at the Co-op . . .
except that shoppers like you
own the Co-op . . .
You get what you want—
and you share the profits too.
That's why we call it
your Co-op.

"